WITH REG.

MR TREWIN

A WOMAN'S SURVIVAL

A WOMAN'S SURVIVAL

Dionne Trewin

The Book Guild Ltd
Sussex, England

First published in Great Britain in 2001 by
The Book Guild Ltd
25 High Street
Lewes, East Sussex
BN7 2LU

Typesetting in Times by
IML Typographers, Birkenhead, Merseyside

Printed in Great Britain by
Bookcraft (Bath) Ltd, Avon

A catalogue record for this book is available from
The British Library.

ISBN 1 85776 615 6

CONTENTS

ACKNOWLEDGEMENTS

I would like to thank my three sons, Kenworthy, Kingsley and Gerald, whom I love very much, for giving me the encouragement and mental support that I needed, and which I could only get from them. I also want to thank my very beloved niece Mrs Sarah Haddow for her moral support, which she gave me unreservedly.

In October 1994 I met and married William John Trewin, whom I call the lion heart, the man who changed my life and made it possible for me to write this book. I want to thank to thank him for his encouragement and moral and financial support, and for giving me permission to add his life story at the end of this book. I want to thank him also for the patience he showed when I was writing and asking him questions, and for never pushing me to write when I did not feel like writing, sometimes for days or weeks. I would like to add that it was a blessing to meet and marry him, for it was the best thing that ever happened to me.

PREFACE

At the time I decided to write about my life, I had been very lonely, and suddenly thought I would put everything on paper so that in years to come my children and relations would understand some of the sufferings I went through. My children were now grown up and living away in different countries, and though we would talk to each other on the telephone, it was not the same as being with them. When they visited me they were proud of my achievements, I was now a property owner with a two-bedroomed flat in London. I was working for a private hospital on night duty for seven nights on and seven nights off. During my nights off I would work an extra six nights with nursing agencies in other hospitals in and out of London, going anywhere they asked me to go, sometimes getting lost at night in the middle of London. I had been working for the last seven nights as a nurse, so I decided I was not going to do anything that day, for I was tired and happy to be at home. I had no social life, and I had not thought about going out. I decided that the time was right to write about my life; I thought I had seen and done everything and I wanted my children to read about what I had gone through, after my death.

BOOK ONE
DIONNE

1

Early Years in Rhodesia

I was born in 1937 in what was then Southern Rhodesia. My parents were officers of the Salvation Army thus we were considered an upper-middle-class family. I was one of five girls, with one brother and two stepbrothers. We were very close, and as we grew up we never knew that we had different mothers. We were not told, and it was a subject which was never mentioned. I found out about this when I was in my late teens. I was devastated and cried myself to sleep, but thank goodness, nothing changed in our family relationships; we were treated the same and this made life easier for all of us. We loved each other, and we were all sent to the Salvation Army schools for our education.

My father had been married twice before. He and his first wife had had a son, but she died in childbirth. Later he remarried and had another son, but he and his second wife never got on well, and he sent her away to her parents. The son grew away from him, and my father did not visit him or contribute to his upkeep. My father later met my mother, and after they got married they decided to go for training in the Salvation Army as officers. When they were junior officers they had their first daughter, Esther. They were then posted to their first corps, where they were to be in charge of a school. Many children used to come for Sunday school, and one Sunday morning my mother noticed a boy who was the spitting image of my father. Later, she asked him about this little boy. He quickly agreed that he could be the son he had not wanted to know when he was born. He was now seven years old and was already late in starting school. My mother decided to take the boy into the family and though my father was against this, she told him that she was going to take him anyway, whether he liked it or not. My father could never refuse her anything, because he loved her very much, and so at the same time she took in my father's first son. Now my mother had two stepchildren and her own little girl. They grew up together as two brothers and a sister.

We were a close, neat family. We all had a good education. My bothers and sisters all married well. When the time came for me to get married, I had been dating a young man for a few years. He was studying at the same college as me, and I had met him through his sister. It was instant love when we first met. We were both young; I was 20 and he was 21 years old. My mother thought we were too young to marry, but no one was going to stop us – we had decided to spend our lives together. We were engaged in the same year as my elder sister got married, and a year after that we were married. My mother began to love him, and that was wonderful for me. My father had died when I was 10 years old and my mother, being a single mother now, was very protective towards me. Since I was her last child, I was spoilt; all my brothers and sisters treated me like a child. I liked having everything done for me (such as cooking, washing and ironing), but I was prepared to look after my husband and our home. Simon and I had known each other for seven years and were at the same college, he was two classes above me. We got married in the Salvation Army, with many people coming from far and near to witness our marriage, and guests dancing until the early hours of the morning. In my church in those days no alcohol was allowed, but a few young people were drinking without their mothers' awareness.

After our wedding we stayed with Simon's aunt. She had a house in one of the African high-density areas, and was willing to accommodate us since we had no money to pay for rent. She was good to us in a way, for Simon had lost his mother when he was sixteen years old, and this lady, a sister of his father, took over as a mother to him. But I realised later on that what she really wanted was to control our lives and our children's lives. We stayed in her house for three months. By then we were expecting our first child.

My husband was then transferred to Bulawayo, the second largest city in Zimbabwe. The largest was Salisbury, now called Harare.

I was pleased with this transfer, for now we were going to have our own place. We were promised a small house as soon as we arrived; Simon went first to see the place and get acquainted with the area. When my turn came to follow, Simon arranged for me to fly instead of going by train or car, as he thought I might lose our baby, and the flight was only forty-five minutes. I was thrilled to fly as this was my first time to do so, and this made me love my husband more. On my arrival at the airport a company car was waiting for me, driven by a chauffeur as Simon could not drive yet. He had a bicycle which he used to ride to work.

Our small house was nice and clean with one bedroom, a kitchen with the smallest stove I had ever seen, using wood for cooking; and there was a lounge. An outside toilet was a rounded little room made of tin and asbestos, very hot inside. After using the toilet you would fetch water in a bucket to flush it, and you would have to fetch more and more water as needed. What was funny was that people would know just what you had been doing according to how many buckets of water you fetched to flush the toilet.

In those days Africans used to live in compounds and locations away from the white men's houses. The only people who were allowed in a white man's area were the servants; anyone else and they would set their dogs on you and no one would come to your rescue. I remember when my uncle went to look for employment as a gardener, dogs were set on him and he nearly had his private parts torn apart. But for the intervention of the postman, who was black, he would have bled to death. White youths were looking on, and edging on the dogs to be more vicious. He came home in great pain and was taken to hospital, but that was that; nothing was said, because an African was not worth bothering about, and no lawyer would take up a case like that. What was a black man doing in a white man's area?

After we had moved to our small house our first son was born, to much joy. The night before his birth I started having backache and feeling generally unwell, but thought little of it, and we slept until in the early morning when the pain became unbearable. I decided that Simon should take me to the hospital, and because we had no car he helped me on to his bicycle saddle and pushed me to the clinic, where they transferred me to the main maternity hospital for Africans. By this time I was in great pain; I spent the whole following day in labour. My mother and my brother's wife were waiting outside the hospital. My husband had been refused time off by his employer, because an African was not supposed to witness his child's birth unlike a white father.

Our child was born at five in the afternoon; he was a big baby weighing nine pounds ten ounces. I knew it was a boy; I had told everyone that I would have a boy. He did not cry when he came out, for he had the umbilical cord around his neck, and he was tired due to the long delivery. He looked the spitting image of his father, and Simon was proud to have a son and happy. I was not allowed to see him that day, because the hospital staff thought he was tired. I cried myself to sleep, thinking my baby was dead and they did not want to tell me. Early in the morning, although I was sore because I had stitches for a tear, I went in search of my baby. I followed the cries of babies, looking in each cot until I found my treasure lying in his cot peacefully with a name-band around his wrist. But I could have picked him without the name, because he was the image of his father. I then went back to my bed and had the most beautiful sleep of contentment.

My mother had travelled all the way from her home three hundred miles away, and was staying with my half-brother and his wife who were working in that city. When my mother came to visit me and the baby I burst into tears, for I was so happy to see her. I could not stop crying, and she became concerned, thinking that maybe the baby was dead or disabled, until I told her that we were both fine and I was just happy to see her. One week later the stitches were taken out and I was discharged from the maternity hospital; my mother, the baby and I went to our little house. Simon was at work, as he was not allowed to take time off even to take us home. Nevertheless he was happy with our little boy, and could not take his eyes away from him. My mother stayed with us for two months to help with the baby, for she was an experienced lady and I needed her until I was sure that I could care for the baby myself. She was a great help during those early days of my son's life. Today midwives give advice and support after a mother has been discharged, but I had to learn quickly from my mother, and after two months I was able to look after our baby when she left for her home.

2

A Young Wife and Mother in India

Simon wanted to go for further education. I was all for it, for I knew that if he went abroad I would have the chance of furthering my own education. So he started applying to universities abroad, and after some time was accepted by the University of Delhi, in India, to study for a B.Sc. in zoology. Simon wanted to study medicine and become a doctor, but unfortunately was not accepted by the School of Medicine, so he had to take the second-best. The scholarship he had won did not go as far as to include students' wives, so this meant that Simon had to go without our child and me. We talked at length about what we should do; he promised that when he got there he would work hard to find a way for me to follow him, though our child would have to remain behind. It never worried him who would look after his child. On his side of the family there was no one who was prepared to look after our baby for two to three years. I should have seen through him then – that he wanted to go ahead with his life despite having a family who needed him – but I only wanted him to be happy; that was all that mattered to me. Then my sister and her husband agreed to have my baby and me to stay in their house, so I thought that the situation was solved. I did not think of the future, looking back now I see that it created an antagonism between our families later on, when life started changing for the worse in my family.

Simon left for India immediately his scholarship came through and I moved to my sister's house with my baby who was now eighteen months old. We lived with them for one year, and were very comfortable. My sister had a good job as a nursing sister, and her husband was a headmaster of a high school in the city of Salisbury. My mother would come to visit us, but she would tell me that she was not happy with the set-up, that I had been left behind by my husband, and being a young woman, might be tempted to have boyfriends. I understood her concern, but that was far from my mind because I loved my husband too much to think of even talking to other men. My mother did not believe in couples living apart, and there was nothing like divorce in her vocabulary. I decided I was going to go to India to be with my husband. My mother said I was not to worry about my child; she would look after the little boy. She did not want any money from us, she had her pension and she only wanted for me to be with my husband. I then began to approach a few organisations for help with money to be able to go to India. As an African in Rhodesia then I had one out of nine chances for any organisation to help me. A university professor who was a family friend and who knew a few organisations helped me to approach them. We approached the Hindu organisation, which asked me to write a letter to the president of the organisation explaining why I wanted to go to India and how much I would need for the fare. In the letter I quoted two fares, by ship and by air. When I received the reply, they had agreed to sponsor me to go by ship, travelling third class; that was the cheapest fare, at £80 for a single ticket to Bombay. Although they had agreed to give me the money, they thought that as an African I was not fit to travel first or second class, these were for whites and well-to-do Indians. I was just thankful that I had the money to pay for my fare to India.

My husband had been away now for one year and I missed him very much. We wrote to each other regularly, but our letters used to take a long time to arrive; we had no contact by telephone, as today. When the Hindu organisation agreed to sponsor my trip to India, they invited me to meet the president and other members of the organisation. I was excited and apprehensive because I was to give a speech thanking them and explaining to the members why I wanted to go to India and what would I do when I was there. Would I be going to study or would I just be with my husband until he completed his studies? When I gave my speech I could not help my voice shaking with emotion and tears running down my face. I thanked them for their wonderful help, and told them I was going to train as a nurse if I was accepted at one of the schools of nursing. (But that was not to be, as I found out later that it was difficult for Africans at that time to train as nurses in Indian hospitals because of racial abuse. It was better in the universities because there were quite a number of Africans studying there, so that Indians were used to seeing Africans about in the university campuses. But I remember a few times when Indians would stop and stare at us, laughing and calling us names, touching our hair without asking us.)

On the day of my departure for India, I travelled by train from Salisbury to Maputo where I was to embark a ship to Bombay. I was excited, for here I was, a young woman who grew up in central Africa and had never seen the sea. At the same time I was petrified and distraught at leaving our child behind. I knew that my mother would look after him well, but I was going to miss him terribly. I had read books about how huge a sea was, and I kept thinking of what I would do if the boat capsized in the middle of the sea, for I could not swim and thought of how the sharks would come after us. I prayed and prayed to God that the boat would not sink and that I would see my husband, as the train to Maputo made its twelve-hour journey to the quay on the Indian Ocean. We arrived in the evening. When I looked out to the sea I was amazed to see so much water. At the same time I saw the ship which was going to take me to India. Oh! I never thought it would be so big. I and other passengers were asked to leave our luggage to be loaded in a motorboat; passengers would be taken in another. I refused to leave mine behind, for I thought I would not see it again and they let me take it with me; after all it was just one medium-sized case. I could touch the sea water as we were being taken across to our ship which was anchored at sea.

When we reached it I noticed men in white uniforms and caps, the crew and staff; as the passengers were helped aboard they would ask what cabin we were booked in. I was booked in third class and as soon as I told them they quickly lost interest in me and just pointed to where third class was. Third class accommodation in an Indian ship was something to make one very depressed. It appeared like a huge playground on different levels, with bunk beds scattered everywhere, the toilets were dirty, and people were spitting everywhere. I looked at these people, some of them with brown teeth from chewing *pani*, a green leaf, which they chew and then spit on the floor. I felt tears in my eyes; the Indian music, which I had not heard before, was blaring.

I put my case on my bunk and thought to myself how I was going to survive. I felt claustrophobic; I had to try and calm myself down. I thought of going to see the captain of the ship to see if he could let me go back home; but it was too late to do so. I then went up on the deck, which was very nice, clean and with fresh air to breathe. Passengers of all classes and races would mix there. I stayed there for a long time waiting for the ship to start moving, for that was an experience I did not want to miss. I began to feel tired and disappointed because the ship had not moved yet, so I went back to my bunk and slept.

In my sleep I felt a sudden movement, I woke up, wrapped myself in my gown and ran up to the deck and yes, at long last we were moving. I could not see much as it was at night, but I could see frothy water in our wake. I went back to sleep and early in the morning, before breakfast, I was on the deck, and now I could see the Indian Ocean, but no land could be seen. We were now many miles out to sea. I then went to have a wash and went to the dining room, which was situated in a corner of the ship near the cargo where one could not see much of the water. After my breakfast I sat on the deck. I would do the same after every meal. It was very hot and humid in the bunk area; there were curry and vomit smells which I could not tolerate. I did not feel seasick even when the ship at one time was pitching up and down. I was now used to the crew, who knew me as a good sailor. I would find myself the only passenger in the dining room, for most Indians had their own food and most could not tolerate English meals.

We first sailed to Dar es Salaam and were there for a few hours; some passengers went out on the town but I could not see myself finding my way out and back. We then sailed for Zanzibar, and when we docked there, people from the island came on board with fruit, silk materials and other curios to sell. I had heard about coconuts and how one could drink milk from them; I was greedy and bought four. They were fresh plucked from the coconut trees that day, I paid sixpence for them. The man who was selling them made an opening for me to drink the milk from, I put this fruit to my mouth and started drinking the milk. It was a cool, sweetish fluid. I did not like the taste; one mouthful was enough for me. I put them on my bunk bed and watched the other passengers enjoying their coconuts; after drinking they would open the fruit and scoop the white substance into their mouths. I waited for the ship to sail, then took all four coconuts and threw them through the porthole. It never occurred to me to offer them to the other passengers, I suppose because I had not made any friends. The Indian passengers were not forthcoming, and were bewildered by an African woman going to India. What was she going to do there?

After the ship had been sailing for some time, I went to the dining room for supper and during the meal a man came to sit at my table. He started talking to me; I looked at him, surprised to hear a voice speaking to me in very good English, for I had given up expecting anyone to speak to me. He was older than I was, about thirty, (I was twenty-two years old then), a tall and handsome man of a mixed race. I was surprised that he was talking to me, a black woman. In Rhodesia men of mixed race considered themselves almost white, and would never be seen talking to black women other than their mothers. Some mixed-race children even used to divorce their mothers because of their black skin, and some used to banish them to the kitchen to appear as their house-girls. Mixed-race people used to have their own schools, their own suburbs and their own public houses. They were told by the white Rhodesians that they were better than the blacks. So when this man started talking to me I was apprehensive, but I took it as a gesture of friendship and I was grateful to be able to talk to someone after a few days of silence. He appeared to know about ships; he showed me where the bars were, and swimming pools. Unfortunately I could not swim and had never tasted alcohol; also we were third class passengers and not allowed to use those facilities. When we docked in Mombasa in Kenya for four days, he took me out to the market and the town, which I enjoyed very much. There was no feeling of romance between us. We were just being friendly and I was eager to tell him why I was going to India, and about my husband. Maybe I put him off.

On the fourth night we sailed off; and by now I was used to the movement of the ship, and enjoying myself. We docked in the Seychelles in the early morning, and when I went for my breakfast to my joy there were a few African students who had boarded the ship in Mombasa. We greeted each other because we were all black, although from different African countries, and shared the same feeling of fighting against those who thought we were an inferior race. We all went out to the island, and I never saw my mixed-race friend again. He just disappeared.

There were many motorboats coming to the large ship to sell their curios to the passengers, but most interesting to me was seeing so many beautiful girls coming on board to sell themselves to men for money. I had never seen prostitution in my life. When the students went out to the island the next day I did not go with them, and that was when I saw these beautiful black girls touching men's faces and kissing them. It was a shock to me but also an eye-opener.

We sailed on the third day after docking in Seychelles for Rawalpindi, Pakistan. It took us seven days from Seychelles to Pakistan. We docked in Rawalpindi in the morning, stayed on board until late in the afternoon, when we all went out on to the town as by then it was not so hot. It is an over-populated city, with people, cattle and buffaloes all moving together in that intense heat and dust. I was surprised to see women dressed in long dresses, their heads and their faces covered with only slits for their eyes. I felt suffocated just looking at these women, wondering if they were able to breathe. I asked some of the students I was with about this code of dress, and was told that Moslem women are not supposed to show their faces and legs to anybody other than their husbands. We then went in search of a restaurant or a café where we could have a snack and a cup of tea. We went into a café where we asked for tea; it was not the tea I was used to but milky and served in a glass. I had never felt so thirsty and frustrated for want of a good cup of tea. We left that café and looked for a restaurant; this time we found a place where not only was there a good tea but lovely food and an outside dance floor where we could hear western music playing. I felt elated just hearing the beautiful instruments being played. As we all sat outside and listened to the music, one male student asked me for a dance, and from then on I was asked by several men to dance. I thoroughly enjoyed myself, thinking all the time that life was going to be wonderful, as I should soon be dancing with my husband to that kind of music. At twelve midnight we left for our ship and our bunks.

The next day we were sailing for Bombay, the last leg of this long journey, and I was looking forward to seeing my husband, who I knew would be waiting for me when the ship docked. We sailed for seven days, seeing nothing but water. By this time I was excited and at the same time getting tired of the journey and seeing the same people every day, and no land to be seen on the horizon. I was getting depressed with other passengers vomiting and spitting everywhere, and as we got nearer the heat and the humidity became unbearable, the smell worse, until that wonderful morning when I woke up in the early morning and saw the land on the horizon and felt my heart swell. It was beating so fast that I feared I might suffer a heart attack, or faint. It was still too far away for the ship to dock; I thought the ship was moving deliberately slowly, I had packed my case and a handbag ready to disembark the minute the ship docked. I stood on the deck with my two pieces of baggage for a long time in the sweltering heat and humidity, watching the horizon drawing nearer, and the time of my being reunited with my husband whom I had not seen for a long year. I was pouring with sweat by the time the ship docked at Bombay, as I stood there, my eyes scanning through hordes of people for a glimpse of my husband. I panicked at first because there were so many people, so much shouting, made worse by being in languages I could not understand.

After some considerable time I saw him, a lone figure standing there. What a wonderful time that was. When I spotted him I forgot all about going through immigration; I wanted to run to him as soon as the gangway was in position for passengers to walk onto land. I was stopped and told that I had to show my passport and have it stamped. Immediately afterwards I walked down that gangway, almost flying, but at the end of the gangway I encountered hordes of dock porters wanting to carry my luggage for money. It was a very frightening experience, for I panicked and was almost in tears when suddenly my husband was there, holding my arm and telling the porters to leave us alone. We carried my luggage away from the masses of people, with me still waiting for him to take me in his arms and kiss me, but he whispered in my ear that if we were to kiss we would be arrested, as kissing in public was an offence in India. Disappointed, I had to respect the law of the country. We called for a taxi to take us to our hotel, which was near the sea.

At last I was with my husband, and it was like a lovely dream. We kissed in the privacy of our room and talked about the many things that had happened while we were apart. I was shy, as if I was meeting him for the first time. Couples should never be apart for a long time, because they have to get to know each other again, but we soon got to know each other in Bombay, and our second son was conceived there. We had a wonderful time in our seaside hotel; standing on the balcony my breath was taken away by the beauty of the city and the scattered lights on the moving boats. I was proud to be there, standing beside my husband; it was almost like a dream, but it was not. We had dinner, and since we did not drink alcohol, we toasted each other with soft drinks; we went to bed late although we were to leave for Delhi the next day.

In the morning after breakfast we went for a short sight-seeing tour; we could not afford to stay in Bombay for more than one night. I thought I was in a different city from the one I had seen the previous night, not so breathtakingly beautiful, but with millions of people, and beggars everywhere I looked, dirty babies on their mothers' laps, and young children begging with sores on their faces and legs. I was astonished to see such poverty in India and such filth, because in Salisbury the Indians were masters who were supposed to be clean and rich. Although we were poor there were no beggars there. If an African was found in the city begging he or she would be arrested and serve a long jail sentence. When I saw these filthy-looking Indians I could not believe my eyes; this was an amazing revelation. I wanted to write to my mother there and then to tell her what I had seen.

Soon it was time to leave for the station to board our train to Delhi. I just followed Simon; I could not have travelled without him because I would not have been understood by the local people, but Simon, having been in India for a year, knew how to talk to them. At the station there were even more people and beggars, and although I did not have much money, I wanted to give these poor children and their mothers the change I had but Simon told me not to, because, he said some of them were richer than those who went to work.

We managed to board the train to Delhi: a nine-hundred-mile journey. We had bought four huge mangoes to eat on the train. Trains in India at that time were fast running, on broad gauge; the only unfortunate thing about them was that the coaches had no connecting doors, so when one wanted to go to the restaurant car, one had to wait until the train stopped at a station, get out and run to the dining car, stay there until it stopped again, then run back to one's coach. That was what we did, but when we came back we found our mangoes gone: someone had helped themselves to them. We had eaten, so really it did not matter much, but we had a good laugh about it. On the journey I saw women working knee-deep in the rice fields, and ploughing with weird wooden contraptions. It was all still a surprise to me to see Indians in such muddy fields, let alone ploughing.

We arrived in Delhi after twenty-four hours; we took a cab to the flat Simon had found for us. It was nothing to talk about, but it was clean. We were sharing it with a brother-in-law of my sister who was studying medicine, and that made it cheaper for us, but it was just a bedsit and shared bathroom. I did not mind all these restrictions as long as I was with my husband. After two weeks we knew that I was pregnant, because I could not tolerate the smell of rice. I would throw up as soon as I smelled rice cooking somewhere, and that was quite often. I used to sweat all the time because it was so hot in the months of June and July. It would rain at one moment and then suddenly it was as dry as if there had not been any rain. I was lonely during the day when Simon was at the university, but it would be all right in the evening when he was back with me. In the same complex where our flat was there was a young Indian couple who invited us to their flat for tea. The husband wanted his wife and me to be friends since neither of us was working; and I wanted this desperately because then I would not be alone and would have someone to talk to. The only language we could communicate in was English. The husband could speak

English well enough to understand and he would translate what we had said into Hindi for his wife. She had a Ph.D. in Hindi. I was very disappointed that she could not speak English and wished that I could speak Hindi. I realised from that time that English was not the only language to be spoken in the world, as I was given to understand by some English people who came to Rhodesia. I began to respect people who spoke their own language but our friendship never took off because of the language barrier.

I used to stand on our balcony during the day watching all the activities going on outside. I was too nervous to go out there alone, too afraid of getting lost and being unable to find my way home as no one would understand English. Besides, Indians would stare at me and talk among themselves, rather than listen and help. They were not violent people, but the way they would stare at a foreigner and sometimes laugh I considered a very rude behaviour. If Simon was free to take me to the city of Delhi, it was always so nerve-racking that by the time we got back to our flat we would be tired and angry with Indians for staring. The people who used to stare and laugh at us were usually poor and dirty-looking. Most students used to want to lash out at them; we took it for the ignorance of people who had never travelled. In later life I experienced the same staring behaviour in many countries where I have visited and lived.

During that period of my pregnancy I missed my mother and my sisters, or at least another woman to talk to. Fortunately three male students decided to have their fiancées join them to get married in Delhi. I had met one of these young women before in Salisbury. The two of us were based in Delhi, and the other two in Lucknow, a city far away from Delhi. She and I formed a good friendship and saw each other almost on a daily basis, she was also pregnant, with her first baby. We would go shopping and protect each other from the staring and silly questions; so we became stronger, sometimes responding to the Indians who were laughing at us by laughing back at them.

Although as students we had not much money, food was cheap, and only accommodation was expensive. We managed, and we were given two hundred rupees to buy the first essentials for the baby. During my pregnancy we had registered with St Steven's maternity hospital; I had everything prepared and a case packed ready for when I would be taken to the hospital. On the day when my pains started, my husband was at the university as it was daytime. I was alone , there was no telephone and no one I could send to call an ambulance or a doctor. In Delhi there were many general practitioners, but in the position I was in, I could not get to one of them. I had had some experience at home watching my mother who was a village midwife as well as a Salvation Army officer, so I spread a blanket on the floor, sat on it and started to push. This was my second baby so at least I knew what was coming; this time I had no problems and my baby boy was delivered within a short time. I then covered my baby with another blanket I pulled from the bed, which was quite near me; my baby was still attached to the placenta which after a short while I started to push out without any problems. At that point one of the students who was living in the room next to ours came back from the university, and hearing a baby crying called out to me asking what was happening. I called back to him to fetch a doctor, and that the baby was already delivered. A lady doctor came, very surprised that I had delivered on my own and wanting to know where my husband was. She kindly cleaned me up, made me comfortable and advised me to register the baby as soon as possible as Indian officials want babies delivered at home to be registered within the week.

When my husband came home at about six in the evening the baby was one hour old, he was so surprised and so pleased to have another boy. Simon did not make it to register the baby within the week as we were advised; he left it for seven days, then had to lie to the officials about the baby's birthday. Although my son knows that he was born on the fifth, his birth certificate is registered the twelfth. Simon was always putting his education before his family's needs; he kept on saying he was very busy with reading and researching. Now I realise he was selfish, but at the time I was not aware of this.

Although the baby was well and thriving, there were a few difficulties, the weather was very hot and humid and he cried most of the time. At times I would put him in tepid water just to cool him down. The Indians loved my baby, and our landlord gave him an Indian name, the same name as his only son's, Krishna Lal. His daughters would come to take the baby out to show their friends and say that because the baby was born in India he had nice straight hair and fair skin. (African babies often have almost straight hair and fair skin when they are born.)The snake-charmers also came to play for my son. I do not like snakes, but I just paid them and asked them to go away.

When our baby was almost one year old, Simon was very busy with his final examinations, and decided that our son and I should leave for home to give him more time to study. I readily agreed to this suggestion as I was homesick, although I did not want to leave my husband behind in India. We then started to make preparations for our departure by ship. We made all the bookings and to our surprise it was the same ship which I had sailed in on my outward journey. The week we were suppose to leave Delhi my son caught a cold and a terrible cough; we decided that it was better for us to leave. Simon accompanied us to Bombay to board the ship. The train to Bombay was packed to capacity and some passengers were riding outside holding onto the windows. The heat and the smell of human sweat was overpowering and the noise and people spitting on the floor was something I will never forget as long as I live. The baby was sweating, frightened and crying and I was immensely relieved when we arrived in Bombay, in time to board the ship, and said farewell to Simon. We were in the third class, as we had no money for second class. This time it was worse because I had a child who needed more space and was not feeling well. I really thought I was going to lose him aboard the ship; he was coughing, had a high temperature and was not eating. I went to the clinic and the doctor gave him some antibiotics and cough mixture, with very little effect. I prayed every day and night to be able to get home with my baby. I had enquired of other travellers what would happen if my baby died at sea, and they said he would be 'buried at sea'. I could not bear that, so I was determined to take my baby home alive. I would take him on the deck and sing to him until he went to sleep.

One day we went to the dining room for breakfast, and to my astonishment I met the same man who had befriended me on my outward journey. He was very surprised to see me, and with a baby, not looking as smart as I was when he first met me. I told him my baby was ill and that my husband would be coming some time later; I could see the pity in his eyes. To this day I thank God for looking after my baby; his health improved slightly and we docked safely at Maputo.

3

Return to Africa – Zambia

At Maputo we boarded the train for Salisbury, a journey of one and a half days. I was just happy to be on that train home. We managed to travel second class, without sharing with other passengers, which was very nice. First and second class were mostly for whites, but if Africans wanted to travel in those classes and were able to pay they were allowed, for they would not be mixing with white people. They would not be allowed to go to the dining car which was reserved for whites. Waiters would come to take orders for food. My son and I had the compartment to ourselves; he enjoyed crawling and climbing on the bunks and looking out of the window to see the countryside. Our bunks were made up with clean sheets and blankets, and for the first time since we left Bombay we had a wonderful and restful night without the heat and smell of human sweat. At each station, when the train stopped whites would throw sweets at the African children who would run to pick them up, and the whites would laugh, and give their own children more sweets to throw. It was an entertainment or a circus for their children. I watched this behaviour and I felt sick and angry at the whites. I thought to myself I should never have booked to travel second class, and from then on I never did. I would travel by buses, because these were only for Africans; no African would be allowed on buses for whites, which carried a bold sign in front: WHITES ONLY. This sign appeared on toilets, restaurants, hotels and most large stores.

The day we arrived in Salisbury, my mother, sisters and my father in law were waiting for us, with my other son who was now five years old. Although we had not seen each other for two years, he automatically knew that I was his mother, and he came shyly into my arms. I held him as if I would never let him go; I was crying with happiness to see him and promised that I would never leave him again. He had had all my mother's love; he was the apple of her eye. She gave him warmth and affection and I thank her still today. My father-in-law was very happy to see us, especially his second grandson, but he thought we had brought presents and money, for I had two large cases for my son's clothes and mine. We were going to stay with my mother and my sister who had a comfortable home and was a nursing sister at a big hospital in Salisbury. Her husband had gone to Oppenheimer College in Zambia to further his education. My father-in-law was living in a smaller house and had a woman friend, since my mother-in-law had died before I was married. He thought the cases should have been taken to his house and been opened there, so he could see what was inside them. It was very embarrassing; we invited him to come with us to my sister's house so he could see for himself, but he declined. From that time on my relationship with him cooled, for he continued to think there was something from his son that I was hiding from him. Eventually Simon arrived after a year and told him about how difficult things were in India, but he still did not believe him. Simon never bothered about it. He arrived in Salisbury one year later with his B.Sc. degree and we were all happy and proud of his achievement.

I must mention here that now that I was back in Salisbury, I looked at Indians in a different way. Here they were acting as if they were above the African people; and yet they were not wholly to blame for this behaviour. In a way it was the fault of the Boers who had told them that they were better than Africans. I now had a weapon in my hands any time an Indian wanted to act superior to me; I would just mention that I had lived in India for two years and immediately their attitude changed. I started having a few Indian friends, but I could not embrace them wholeheartedly as true friends as long as some Indians were treating my people like slaves. Years later I was not surprised to hear about the Indians being thrown out of Uganda in such a brutal way by the former president Amin. I believe their behaviour towards the Ugandans must have been a factor. In every country they live Indians will always create their own way of living, which I think is very good, if they also try to accommodate to the laws of that country. I am not a politician, and I do not hate Indians, but it is the case that many African countries turned against them after independence. I will also mention here the Indian for whom my father-in-law worked as a butcher, who now talked to me more on the same level as himself. This man was good to my husband; he helped him with college fees whenever Simon's father could not afford to pay them and I would like to thank him for helping Simon through high school.

With Simon now back home with me, my sister left us her house for six months to be with her husband in Zambia, paying six months rent for us as we had no money and no jobs yet, which was extremely good of her. Simon immediately started looking for a job, applying to different companies. He had an honours degree in zoology but the only job he was offered was teaching, which he hated. It was still Rhodesia then, and white employers did not want an educated African sitting in an office and giving orders. There was seldom anything on offer for such Africans except teaching in all-African schools and colleges. They would not be tolerated teaching white pupils.

Zambia by then was free from white minority rule, so we started looking in their job advertisements. The whites in that country were leaving for western countries, or South Africa, because they could not contemplate working together with black people in white-collar jobs. We saw a job advertisement for a fisheries officer; Simon applied for it. After a long wait a reply at last arrived from Lusaka; he was invited for an interview. If he was accepted, that would be our way out of Southern Rhodesia, where black people were never given such jobs. When Simon came back from Lusaka he told us that he had been offered the job. We were jubilant.

We travelled by train to Lusaka and were taken by a chauffeur-driven car to a first-class hotel where we were to stay for a few weeks while Simon attended meetings and was advised about his job. Our hotel was in the centre of Lusaka but because Simon could not drive at that time he had to be driven to and from the office every day. We were a happy family and life was going the right way. After a few weeks, we were informed that we were to be moved to our own station, to manage the fishing there. I should mention that the Fisheries Department was a government department; we were working for the Zambian Government. We were appointed to a very remote but very beautiful area called Kampilimposhi, and were given a four-bedroomed house on the bank of a huge lake. We were also given a four-berth speedboat for our use and the person who managed it. We could take it for picnics, but most of the time it was used by Simon to visit different parts of the lake to meet the fishermen and hold meetings to discuss new ways of fishing. The children and I would sometimes go with him to see the different fishes; they were beautiful and the children loved it. This place was well away from any town, so that I had to learn to make bread. Shopping for groceries was done once a month when our driver would drive us to Lusaka, when we would have a wonderful time, go to a restaurant for a meal and then start back early in the afternoon for it was a long journey. Sometimes we would have a night in Lusaka in a hotel. It was not long before I was pregnant with our third boy.

After seven months at this station we were transferred to another, this time not so far away from a town. This was convenient for our two older boys were now about to start school, one at kindergarten and the other at infant school. Although it was near the town it was still very far to walk to their respective schools, so they would be driven to and fro. They had their own special driver who knew what time to take them and when to pick them up. It was a good life: we had a cook and someone to do the washing and cleaning. We paid them well and gave them good accommodation, not like the way things were when the white masters were in control.

When our older son reached the top class at infant school we had to find a junior school for him. Unfortunately there was none near where we were living, so we managed to get him into a boarding school, very far away. He was seven years old by then, and the first black boy in that school. I was apprehensive, for I was not sure how he would be treated either by teachers or the other students. In a way I was right to be, for sometimes when he came home for school holidays he had scratches on his face, and he would tell me that other boys had been fighting him. But the teachers were nice and understanding. They reassured us that he would come to no harm as they would be monitoring the situation in the students' halls of residence. He used to fly to school for the term, and fly home for the holidays in small planes. I used to be so apprehensive when he was flying in and out; fortunately we were transferred to a larger town where there was a very good school near home.

It was nice to be in a town of that size, we could now buy bread from a bakery and do shopping for home and food essentials. This was a big house; Simon had now been promoted to become the provincial fisheries officer. We soon bought a car, as by now he was able to drive, although he still had a driver to take him to different places, sometimes for up to a week away from home. It was a vast area to cover, and see every chief of the area and headmen. I was now expecting our third child. I had a girl looking after my two boys and a man who used to do the cleaning and the garden. I used to treat them like my relations; at first they were not comfortable with this treatment, as their masters had treated them like animals before independence.

My sister, who had helped us before when Simon went to India, decided to go to Britain for one year to study for an ear, nose and throat [ENT] diploma in Birmingham. She asked us to take her little girl to live with us until she came back, as her family was now based in Lusaka. We were pleased to have her lovely little girl, who was only a few months older than my first boy. I loved her and she loved me; she used to call me mummy. The children would go to school together; at times there would be fights such as all children have. I explained to them that there was no favouritism in my house; they were all my children.

Our third son was born in that town, and in the house, as I was too late to go to hospital; but by a most wonderful chance, my mother had arrived the previous week to visit us, so she was the midwife. The hospital was notified in the morning for the doctor to come and check on both the baby boy and myself, and we were pronounced well. My mother was so good to us, bathing and looking after the baby while I was still weak, making sure that I had a nutritious diet and helping me with my daily baths, My mother was a wonderful woman, full of love and warmth, one of the best mothers in the whole world. She did not do this service only for me, but for all her children.

Presently I began to get my strength back and started to look after the family cooking. I also started going to women's clubs, and ended up being the president of one club organising sports and cooking classes. The women loved it and their men appreciated what we were doing. We stayed in that town for two years; during that time I passed my driving test and I used to take my children to town for shopping, as Simon was always on trips in the wilds. That gave me independence, for I no longer had to wait for the driver to take us to town.

When the time came for us to be moved we were sent to the capital city Lusaka; we were delighted. We were given a four-bed roomed house situated in beautiful gardens. After a year Simon was appointed as an adviser to the minister of agriculture and wild life. He would travel with him abroad or write notes of what the minister was to say at meetings. Our two boys were now grown-up little boys, but our youngest was still very young. My sister's little girl had returned to her parents after her mother had come back from the UK. Simon was then offered the chance to study at the University of Liverpool for an M.Sc. on freshwater fishes.

4

England and Nursing Training

We decided that I should also take this opportunity to go with Simon and do some further education. I decided to go for home management or nursing. Simon later decided that it was not good that we should go together, because of the children. He wanted to leave me again with my sister and her family. My sister was now working at the Lusaka General Hospital, and my mother was helping her with her children. Simon told me that people in Britain would not want children in their homes, or to rent rooms to families with children, because they thought they would make a noise and vandalise their premises, especially if they came from what they called the 'third world' (a phrase I do not understand even today). Simon was right, as I would find out later.

However I was determined that I was not going to be left behind as I was when he went to India. The children and I stayed behind while he went first; he would look for somewhere for us to live. He wrote to us to say he was having difficulties finding a place for us, but I put my foot down and said I was not going to leave my children to be looked after by my old mother again. He later agreed that we should book our flight to the UK.

Simon had said he would meet us at Victoria Station when we arrived, as Heathrow Airport was too far for him, coming from Liverpool. We were so happy to see him, although there was no real happiness on his face. But there again he was never a person to show emotion; moments were rare when he would show pleasure; he always had a serious-looking face. He took us to a bed-and-breakfast, stayed with us for a short time. and announced that he was going back to Liverpool as he had classes the next day. He seemed to be saying to me: it is up to you, girl; now get on with it, you wanted to come. Before I left home I had been given a letter of introduction to an organisation based in Golders Green, a group of Africans from the then Rhodesia living in Britain courtesy of the British Government. These people were against the Smith régime; they would help anyone who needed help from that country. When Simon left us I was lost, stuck with boisterous boys in a small room. I could not take them out, for I was scared; it was all new to me. I phoned this organisation; the man who answered had a fatherly voice, so I introduced myself and the children, explaining my predicament. He said he would come to see me the next day and do what he could about the situation we were in. I went to sleep relieved.

The next day after breakfast he arrived at our hotel and asked me a few questions, like who I was, who were my parents, my husband's name, where he came from, and what he was studying at Liverpool University. I answered all these questions. He was not very impressed with my husband's handling of his family. He offered to take us to a house in Golders Green, where most of the students from Rhodesia were living. I explained this to the children, and they were very happy to leave this confined accommodation. We left with this man who was the head of the students and a well-known political figure in the Zimbabwe political union. We were given the largest room available where four of us could sleep in a king size bed. I would go downstairs to the kitchen to cook meals for the children and myself. It was not the best solution, but we were free to do what we wanted and to go out for walks; we were with people from home, and once the children were in bed, I would go to the lounge and mix with the other students. We would talk, laugh and discuss ways to help each other in this foreign country. We talked about going to college or getting work during our free time from college.

I contacted Simon to let him know what I had done about accommodation and to give him our telephone number, but I can truthfully say he never phoned us. I would phone each time I wanted to talk to him; I missed him so much, and the children would ask when we would be going to see Dad. I would explain to them that Dad was busy studying and would be coming to see us as soon as he was free. I then talked to the man who had first given us this accommodation. I said to him that it was not fair to the other students having kids there running around everywhere, when what they needed was to concentrate on their studies and their jobs. I needed either to go to college or to get a job. He was a very understanding person and to this day I think of him as my saviour. (Much later, when he was a judge in Zimbabwe, he was killed in a car accident. I was devastated, and so were many people whom he had helped when he was in London.) He said to me that the only thing I could do was first to look for foster-parents to look after the children five days a week, while I would have them when I was off work or college. It was a good idea but I did not want to part with my boys. Still, there was no other way I could leave the children alone. Two were now going to school and the other was due for school. He helped me to look for a good family who would take three little black boys into their home. We found a family in Tulse Hill. It was not the cleanest of homes but they were warm people who had their own two children, older than mine. I could see they needed money and I paid them forty pounds a week, which was expensive at that time. I wanted my boys to be looked after well, and I had enough money to pay for them. I then went to college in Holborn for my A-levels. I really enjoyed that, and meeting people from all over the world. I would go and take my children out for a meal, and during the holidays we would go for a day away by coach, and they used to love that.

Still I was not happy with the situation, so when I finished at Holborn College I reviewed the situation. I decided to move to the north of England, as I thought it a more relaxed and friendly part of the country. I talked to a man who was a student at York University and also a political figure in exile. He had a house, but was not living in it; there were only two students living there and a lot of space. He then said if I wanted to go there I was welcome. I thanked him, and my boys and I left for York at the end of 1967. We were free there: we occupied the whole ground floor and my boys could go out to play. People were very nice; the two students were girls and they were good to the children. We became friends; even today we are still friends. The school was very near, and a nursery school was just round the corner.

I still wanted to see my husband. I phoned him to let him know of our move to York and asked him if I could go and see him. He made a few excuses, saying that he was busy and did not see why he should waste money paying for a hotel, and promising to come and see us when he was not so busy. I begged; I told him I really missed him, that I would just come for the day, not spend a night with him. If he could just meet me at Liverpool Lime Street and spend a few hours or have a meal together, after that I would take my train back to York. He agreed to this; oh I was happy. I told the boys that I was going to see their dad. By now they were not that interested. They never asked questions. One of the students offered to look after the boys; she even said if I wanted to spend a night there I should just phone to let her know, and it would not be a problem.

When I arrived at the station Simon was there to meet me, and I was very happy to see him. He did not look as happy, but I did not care, for here was my husband and that was all that mattered to me. He quickly said to me he had decided that we should spend a night together, as it would be a waste of time and money to come and go back the same day. I was so happy that I could not contain myself. He had booked bed and breakfast at a small and not so clean hotel, but I did not mind at all. He was never a man for communication and jokes. We went to bed, and to be honest I do not think there was any wonderful lovemaking. The next day he took me to the laboratory where he was working on his research into growing fish, then to the University dining hall where we had a meal. After that we had nothing to say to each other. Really I wanted to go to my children and he wanted to go back to his work, so he took me to the station and I went back to York. We still cared for each other, but he had his work to do, and I had to look after the children while he achieved whatever he wanted in life. I should have seen how he was, but I was in love with him and wanted him to be the best educated man so I could be proud of him and show him off to the world. What I did not realise was that what he was doing, he was doing only for himself.

I decided to apply to go into nursing and in the meantime I was going to get a job. I worked in a department store as a sales assistant, and was quickly accepted for training as a nurse in

Scarborough teaching hospital. I wanted to be near the sea. While I was still waiting to leave York, Simon came to see us and we all stayed in a bed-and-breakfast. The next day he left for Liverpool and we did not hear from him for two months, when a letter came from Zambia explaining that he had not had time to come and see us before his departure. I felt let down and embarrassed – at least he could have phoned to let me know that he was going. I forgave him, however, as I thought he could not help it, and that maybe his employers wanted him as quickly as possible. I told the boys that their father had to go back to Zambia.

It was time now for me to leave for my training in Scarborough. I had to find a family to look after my boys. This family I found was not good to them; their older child used to stamp his foot on my smallest boy's feet, and the bigger boys were woken in the morning to go and buy bread and milk before they went to school. I wrote to their father explaining what was happening; he quickly sent tickets for them to fly to Zimbabwe. I was really grateful to him for taking such prompt action. When I went to get my boys, I told this family that they were cruel, and showed them my son's feet – of course they denied it. It was the happiest day of my life when the children flew back.

I had only two and a half years of my course to complete before I could go back home and be with my family.

During my second year of training Simon wrote to inform me that he would be passing through England on his way to Yugoslavia with the Minister of Fisheries and Wildlife for a conference in that country, and would have a few days with me before he joined the minister in Yugoslavia. I was the happiest woman on earth; he was coming to Scarborough. I wanted him to see me in my nurse's uniform which I was so proud of; I wanted him to see a housewife changed to a professional wife, who still loved him very much. I booked us into a hotel by the sea, and when he arrived I could see in his face how proud he was of my changed outlook. I took him the next day to the hospital to show him around. I had requested a week off so I could be with him. After two days in Scarborough we left for London where we went sightseeing and spent two nights. I bought him a nice jacket which he liked very much. On the third day he flew to Paris as he wanted to see that city for a day before joining his colleagues in Yugoslavia. I took my train back to Scarborough a happy woman and well refreshed; my friends at the hospital teased me but were happy for me as well.

Simon had informed me that the boys were doing well, and I was pleased about that. They had written me some funny and lovely letters which I read over and over again. They wanted children's Corgi books, toy cars and Manchester United shirts. I bought most of the things they asked for and gave them to their father to take home. I then put everything in to my studies, for I wanted to go home as soon as my results were satisfactory. Since the day Simon left England for Paris and Yugoslavia, I barely heard from him again. When I phoned him he sounded pleased, but when I asked him why he never wrote he said he was busy, as he was now in a very high position. In my third and final year there were still no replies to all the letters I wrote to him.

One morning after night duty as we were going to our residence, I got a letter from his cousin, a young lady who used to like me very much when I was in Zambia. She told me that my husband had a girlfriend from Yugoslavia and she was living with him. They were seen everywhere together, and he introduced her as his wife. The children were not happy; she was making them clean their rooms although there was someone employed to do the housework; their rooms smelt of urine as no one was bothering to wash for them. They had been to talk to the Yugoslavian embassy about their engagement and to ask if the ambassador could marry them. Simon's cousin went on to tell me that all my pictures had been removed from the house, and that he had bought her a new car.

As I read that letter I felt faint; the other girls with me were concerned, for they could see that I was not looking well – was some loved one very ill at home? I said no, it was something even worse but I did not tell them what the problem was for I felt ashamed. I excused myself from my friends and made a beeline for matron's office, for I thought she was the only one I could talk to; she was a motherly lady whom I respected very much. When I went in I burst into tears. The poor lady did not know what to do or say; she let me cry till I was ready to tell her, then listened to the end. She asked me what I wanted to do, and I asked her for time off to fly to Zambia to sort out the problem, otherwise I would not be able to concentrate on my studies. I asked for two weeks but I had only two months to go to my finals. She said if that was what I wanted to do, I would by all means be allowed to go for two weeks, but she would like me to come back. I thanked her and went to my room to pack a few clothes for my stay in Zambia.

5

Marital Strife

I caught a train to London and went to a friend's house where I booked a flight. I was lucky to get a seat on Egypt Airways to Dar es Salaam, then on Kenya Airways to Zambia. Unfortunately my connection was not smooth. We were too late to connect with Kenya Airways, so we had to stay the night in Dar es Salaam, where we were given five-star accommodation in a hotel looking over the sea. I was still feeling cold and unwanted, thinking of how I was going to deal with the problem at hand. I went for supper on the balcony of the hotel overlooking the Indian Ocean, and it was so beautiful that on an impulse I ordered the most expensive meal of lobster and salad, to be paid for by Egypt Airways. I had never eaten lobster; when it was served I was horrified to see the shape of it there on my plate, and I asked the waiter to take it back and scoop out the flesh for me. After my meal I took a bottle of Afri-coco, a drink made of wild fruits, very sweet and potent. I wanted something to help me to sleep that night for I felt lonely and angry, but I did not realise how intoxicating the drink was – the after-effects were that I slept on the floor fully clothed until morning. Before I left London I had phoned Simon, asking him if it was true that he had a woman living with him. He said people must have seen him with his doctor who was a lady, but I knew he was lying. I went on to ask if I were to come there, would I find this whole tale to be not true? He said I would find nothing wrong. I did not tell him I was arriving sooner than he thought.

I arrived in Zambia at midday. I had no one to meet me as no one knew I was coming. I took a taxi to my house to find only the cook. We knew each other and he was happy to see me, but nervous. I told him not to worry and asked him where the happy couple was? He said they had gone into town so I asked him when they came back not to tell them that I was in the house. I need not have bothered for when they arrived he ran outside to let them know I was there. Before they arrived I had seen that all my pictures and the children's pictures were gone. I had seen the boys' rooms, filthy and smelling of urine. After cleaning them I sat down and waited.

When they came in Vera, his girlfriend from Yugoslavia was ahead of Simon, screaming at me what did I want and who was I? She turned to Simon and asked him if he knew me. Simon said he had never seen me before. I was so surprised and angry that he could deny he knew me, that I went for this screaming woman. Simon was saying to me in my language that she was a madwoman whom I should not fight as she would destroy everything in the house. I had never fought anyone before in my life, but this time I thought I would fight them. They quickly piled into their car and drove off to a hotel. When the children came back from school, they were so pleased to see me. We cried together, I gave them a bath, changed their clothes and gave them a good meal. After that I was calm and thinking of what I was going to do. I put my children to bed. They were happy that night for they had their mother to talk to and tell them stories. They told me quite a lot about their father and Vera, I reassured them, although my heart was in turmoil.

Later I called my cousin, who immediately came to be with me and to give me moral support. She was devastated when she heard what had happened, and decided to stay with me for as long as I wanted her, or until Simon came back and decisions were made about our future. I was now wondering if I should abort my nursing career, or go back to England and complete my training. I thought that if Simon came back, I would definitely return to England, for he could look after the children for the few months until I qualified, when I would come home and take care of my children. With my qualification I would be able to be independent if there was a divorce. I still loved Simon and if he had come back to me and said he was sorry about the whole affair I would have forgiven him.

The next day my cousin and I went to see him at his office, because I needed money to buy food for the children and myself. We walked (although it took us almost an hour to get there), as he had left not one of the cars. When we got there I saw Vera's car outside his office, and I knew then that she was in there with him. Simon had an English secretary, (of whom I later heard Vera was jealous), and I asked her if I could see my husband. She told me he was busy – I suppose she had been told not to allow me to see him. I said I was going in anyway, whereupon she became very abusive and tried to fight me out of the office. Simon, who had meanwhile appeared, never said a word, but stood there looking down. Thinking I had better resist the woman, I pulled Vera outside the office. Then for the first time I noticed that she and Simon both wore identical rings on their third fingers. I had bent her finger back, asking her to drop the ring, when Simon came out of his office telling me to leave the ring as it was given to her by her father. I asked, why were the rings identical? He was not able to tell me and I knew that he was lying. Many people by now were standing outside watching this fight between the wife and the mistress. Simon's boss tried to talk to me; he had been astonished to learn that Simon had a wife and three children.

When we got back to the house I went to collect the children from school and we had dinner together, and spent the rest of the day playing around and cooking – just like the old times, minus the father of the house. In the evening when we were sitting in the lounge, we heard a car drive up to the house. We all thought it was Simon coming back to us; the children ran to the windows and drew the curtains. To their astonishment it was Vera paying us a visit. Vera came to the door and to my dismay I saw that she was holding in her hands a long steel car steering wheel lock. One could see she was in fighting mood. Instantly I became so angry that I began shaking and sweating. I got hold of her weapon and took it away from her, then marched her to the main bedroom, which they had locked, and demanded that she unlock the door. When she hesitated I slapped her so hard she fell, and I went for her, tore her clothes off and locked her up in the bedroom. I ran to the kitchen and came back pulling the kitchen hose after me, unlocked the door and as she tried to come towards me I sprayed her with hot water. I started to whip her with the hosepipe. Then I must admit that I am not proud of what I did to her, but I was so angry that she had taken my husband and humiliated me. Simon was to blame as well, for he lied to her, saying that he had no family, and she took him at his word.

The fight went on for a long time, and by the time I let her go she had no clothes on and bruises all over her bottom. I went inside my house and closed the door. It was not long before I heard another car driving up towards the house. This time it was the police, whom Vera had met as she was running away. They had put her in the car and covered her with a blanket. They knocked on the door and began asking me questions: who was Simon's legal wife, could they see our passports. I handed them mine, and they informed Vera that I was the wife of this man we were fighting for, and told me to come to the police station the next day. I had broken Vera's front teeth during our fight.

Next day I made sure I was well dressed for the interview with the police, but I was trembling inside when I was ushered into the office of the chief of police. He asked me several questions, and told me that I was charged with grievous bodily harm, which could carry a seven year prison sentence but he was going to let me go, because I must have been provoked beyond control to find another woman in my house. Since I was still in training in England, he advised me, more in a fatherly way than as a policeman, that my husband was not to be trusted, and it would be better for me to qualify and be financially independent, if I decided to come back to Africa. I felt better after this interview, but when I came out I found Vera in the foyer, presumably waiting to hear if I was going to be sent to prison, and outside the police station Simon was waiting for Vera. I walked past with my head held high.

I had now to arrange for my cousin to remain at the house with the children until Simon came back. I was very worried about leaving my children, but had decided to go back to Britain to complete my training so as to be sure of a secure future life alone. After making these arrangements and talking to my children to reassure them, I left for Britain. Although I still hurt within my heart, I resolved to look to the future and make something good for my children and myself.

6

Return to Nursing, and Independence

When I arrived at my school of training, I went to see the matron who was pleased to see me back. It was a struggle to get into studying, but I went at it steadily. However, I could not sit for my finals that year, for I knew that I was not ready and would definitely fail. I worked hard for the next year's finals, and it paid, for I got through. I was very happy with this achievement and decided to stay there for one more year, working to pay back the kindness shown to me during my problems. I then left for Manchester, where a very good friend of mine was working as a nurse. We had qualified the same year and were like sisters. We became inseparable for many years to come. She had gone through the same problems with her husband as I had. We shared a flat and had some very good times when we had found our feet after the traumas we had experienced.

It was very difficult for me to get into a relationship with a man. I found myself hating men, especially those from my country, and I distanced myself from them for a long time. My friend was not as bad as me, and went on dates. We would go to parties and dance all night, but I would not let any man tell me he loved me. The word love was a joke to me then. A few years later I started dating, but not seriously. Maybe I still thought Simon would contact me and tell me he loved me. I think I would have gone back to him, because my mother and sisters wanted us to patch up the marriage. It never happened, and my friend kept telling me to forget him. After some considerable time I went out with a very nice man, a divorcee from Nigeria who was studying to become an accountant at the University of Manchester.

I lived in Manchester for more than ten years. I then went to America where my sister and her family were living. She had persuaded me to work there, but, after a short time I came back. I could not get used to the American way of living; I was used to England. All this time I did not want any communication with my mother, because she would tell me to come home and go back to my husband. She was so frustrated by my silence that she considered asking the Salvation Army to look for me. She was on the point of doing so when I contacted her and told her I was well and thinking of coming home for a holiday. I moved to London, where after a year, I received a letter from Simon, asking me to come home. He was still in Zambia with the children, but thinking of going back home to Zimbabwe. There was no apology, just an announcement of what he had decided to do. I decided that for the children's sake I would go and see what it was all about. I left for Zambia.

Simon met me at Lusaka airport; when I came near him I felt there was nothing between us. If there ever was going to be we would have to work at it damn hard. We had moved away from each other and I was no longer the naïve woman who used to kiss the ground he walked on. We drove home and a very nice home it was too, on a hundred-acre farm, with vegetables, a chicken-run and plenty of eggs, men working on the farm and also three cars in the driveway. I took all this in but was not impressed; I was chiefly happy to see my children, who had grown up. The two older boys were now in secondary school and the youngest was at the end of his primary school. I was taken out to dinner that evening of my arrival, but Simon and I really had nothing to say to each other. We talked mostly about the children. I was dreading going to bed when we went back to the house. Eventually I went and saw the sheets were rumpled as if two people had shared the bed the previous night. The neighbours told me that Simon's girlfriend had left the day I arrived. We shared a bed that night but nothing happened.

I stayed with my family while Simon made all the preparations to go back to Zimbabwe. We were going to sell the farm, and I would remain for a while winding up the sale while he went to start the new job as a lecturer at the University of Zimbabwe. I had decided that our eldest son should go to university and had asked my sister in New York to take him, so that he could go to the university there. I wanted our son to go to America, not Rhodesia, which still had a racist government. So our eldest son left for America and I remained with the two younger boys, while Simon went to South Africa to collect his new Mercedes Benz car. I then started to try and sell the house but was offered much less than the house was worth, so after all I decided to let it for a while.

The two boys had to go to Zimbabwe to meet their father. He had decided that they should travel by road, though there was still a bitter war raging and people were being killed. I accompanied the boys to Victoria Falls. I had a lot of Zambian money with me, to see the boys through with their fares, but this money was worth almost nothing – one person told me that it was like toilet paper. My youngest son was now hungry, hot and crying. I felt helpless, for I could not buy even an ice cream for them. No one wanted the Zambian Kwacha. I then remembered the friendly Indian who had helped Simon through college. I thought I would approach one of the Indian businessmen in Victoria Falls and ask if I could phone him, as I was sure they would know each other. I was lucky, for when I had explained the problem he asked to talk to the businessman in Victoria Falls. Yes, they knew each other well; he asked him to give us Rhodesian dollars, which he did. We were now happy; we had food and money for the fares. I then started looking for transport to take the boys to Bulawayo, and on to Salisbury. Even today I tremble to think what could have happened to my boys on the way – they could have been killed or raped. However, they arrived safely.

Simon met them at the railway station and took them to his aunt, who lived in a high density area, where the boys were devastated by an environment which they were not used to. The aunt used to have people coming to drink at her house, as well as prostitutes who used to go there to look for men. I was very angry about this when I heard of it. Later I found out the reason for it – he did not want them with him as he had a woman in his life, an uneducated girl from Maputo, who was already pregnant with their child.

I eventually sold our property for twice as much as we were

initially offered. During my stay at the farm I had our van stolen, so I had no transport to take myself to town. I was on my own at the farm except for my cook and an Alsation dog. It was a lonely, dangerous place. My mother used to say she was sure that Simon hoped I would be killed there, to make things easier for him. But I survived. However, one night as I was reading a book in bed, I heard a scratching noise coming from the lounge. I got out of bed and there by the window was a man trying to open it through a hole he had made in the glass. I was terrified so I ran back to my bedroom and took a big stick which I used to keep there for self-defence. When I got back to the lounge the man was still there, so I pointed the stick towards him as if it was a gun. He ran away for he could not see properly in the dark and thought I was going to shoot him.

The day I went to sign for the transfer of the deeds to the new owner I got the shock of my life. The solicitor gave me the deeds to read and said that the money had been paid. I then signed and waited for him to give me the cheque from the sale of the property, but instead he thanked me and said that was all he needed from me. My husband had told him not to give me the cheque, but to let me sign first, for if he had told me beforehand I would have refused to sign. When I got out of that office I was robbed of all strength to fight. I had never intended to take the money for myself, but I needed money for the fare home to Zimbabwe, and to transport furniture and other personal effects. I went home and looked around me, and thought I had to sell everything in the house to be able to fly home, and so I did.

I had phoned Simon to meet me at the airport, but when I arrived he was not there. My mother and sisters met me and I had to go with them to my nephew's flat, where everyone was staying. Many people had left their rural homes, due to the Smith's regime killing the villagers. The next day I went to the university to try and talk to Simon, mostly about finance and the children, as we needed somewhere to stay, but he refused to meet me. His boss told me he had gone into town. I went back to the flat where I was staying, and with the little money I had I started looking for accommodation. I found a place near town where I could walk to look for jobs in the city.

My second son was staying with me and looking for a school to go to. I managed to have him taken into a prestigious, formerly all-white school. They were starting to take Africans and because he could speak English well, having stayed in England and started his education there, he had a passport to the white world. We went for an interview with the headmaster who was very pleased, if not shocked, to interview such a smart young African. He asked about England and other issues and by the time we left the office my son had been accepted. One thing we did not think of was the reception he would get from the white boys. I had arranged for him to board while I was trying to put my life together. I paid the fees, as his father would not hear of it. When he started going to Prince Edward he was met with antagonism from the white boys, who wanted to fight and call him names. He started fighting them and I was called in by the headmaster to be told that my boy was beating and fighting other boys. I said the headmaster should ask all the boys why my son was fighting and that my son had told me that the white boys were insulting him. I then decided that he should stop boarding and live with me, but still I would find that he had bruises each time he came home. As he was the only black boy in the school it became very difficult for him; later, when other black boys joined the school the situation became tolerable. My youngest son was attending school at St George's and living in. It was a Roman Catholic school, and they were much better in their attitude towards black students.

During my time of looking for a job I met a young lady who was working with the Zimbabwe Broadcasting Corporation. She took me under her wing and we would do programmes about health and beauty for African women, for I had studied health and beauty, besides nursing, in Manchester. This gave me a little money. We would appear on television and talk about black make-up and styles of dress. I enjoyed that very much, until Simon saw me on the screen, and was not pleased. He came to the Z.B.C and met my producer, saying he had been looking for me, and could he give him my address? My producer refused, but when I arrived the next morning I was told that my husband had been looking for me, and looked angry, so it was better that I should terminate my employment. Fortunately, however, I had a cousin who was a professor at the University of Zimbabwe, who used to give talks on the radio. He would ask people from all walks of life to talk about subjects such as African medicine, or African ways of living. He asked me to talk about life in England, and I would broadcast twice a week. This helped to pay for my rent and school fees for my son at Prince Edward School. I was still looking for a better and permanent job, and one day I answered an advertisement for sales personnel with Berkshire International, who were based in Harare. It was a company which made ladies' tights and underwear; the factory was in Bulawayo, so that if one was accepted she would be sent there for one month's training. I wanted this job so much and thought of it as my last resort, for I was desperate. I was called for an interview at which I felt quite at home, for I was used to talking to white people. I told them I had lived in England for twenty years, and that besides being a nurse I was a health and beauty specialist.

A few days went by and then I received the letter I was waiting for – yes, I had been accepted. I had to go to Bulawayo by plane for the training. There were three of us; we were to be assessed during our training and two were needed out of the three. We were booked in a hotel and had a wonderful time being fetched and brought back to our hotel in a company car – we were beginning to see how the whites had enjoyed the facilities we had not been supposed to know about. It was a tough training, as we all wanted to be chosen for the job, and one lady had an advantage over the other two of us in that she could speak two local languages, Shona and Ndebele. After our training she was given the job of sales representative, and a company car. I was disappointed, but I was given the other job as a company hostess and receptionist. I was also told that because of my good English they were to move a white lady, who had previously held this position, to another department.

I started work on the following Monday; I was the only black there until two other women joined the company as secretaries. Although I was now employed, I still had to settle my marriage problems. It was going to be nasty before I could be free from my husband. One day my sister and her husband decided to hold a party for their friends in the Zimbabwe/Rhodesia Government, as my brother in-law was Minister of Finance. I was invited, with my mother; the party started at eight in the evening. I dressed up in a long, ivory, flowing dress, and was looking forward to enjoying myself. After the guests had gone we settled down to sleep, not knowing that the police special branch had been looking for me at my nephew's house

7

A Political Prisoner

They had surrounded the house armed with machine guns, and arrested my brother-in-law and nephew. It had been alleged that I had brought guns into the country to kill Muzorewa and his cabinet members. When they did not find me there they came to my other brother in-law, the Minister of Finance, and found me there. I remember the loud knock on the door and the dog barking. When we opened the door I saw two white men holding guns and demanding to see me. I was completely surprised by it all, and then scared, because I knew that they could shoot me as they had so many people during that time. I knew I had done nothing and had no intention of killing anyone, but somehow, because I had come from outside the country, they thought I was against them. The commander of the army had received a letter from someone saying I was a threat to the government. It later emerged that General Walls was married to a woman who unfortunately had a name very similar to mine. The police demanded that I should be taken to the police station. My sister and my mother begged them not to take me; my son was devastated. But, my brother-in-law never came out to protest on my behalf – I suppose he wanted to keep his job. It was cold and I had nothing warm to wear, only my flimsy evening dress. I was taken to the central prison in Harare and thrown into a cell. I was appalled for I had never been inside a jail and I was among drug addicts, prostitutes and murderers. We were woken up very early in the morning for a breakfast of uncooked sadza (a Zimbabwean staple food) which I would not normally consider eating at five in the morning. After breakfast we were marched to the conference room, without shoes. It was cold, and our underwear had been taken away in case we tried to commit suicide by strangling ourselves with it. In the conference room the police read notes about each prisoner, stating why they had been arrested; after that we were led back to our cells.

At midday I was called out by a policeman to an office for interrogation. There were three white policemen sitting behind a desk, all looking at me as if I was something that had crawled out of a hole. I was told to sit on a chair with one officer standing behind me. I was told I had been arrested because they had received a letter informing them that I had brought guns to kill government ministers. I asked who had sent the letter, but they did not like me asking questions, so I was slapped on both sides of my face, so hard that it started to swell up immediately. I did not cry, for I thought they would rejoice to see my tears, but I was so angry with them that I could have fought them. I was told that they had changed my name to Alice, so that my family would not be able to find out where I was being held. This was a common practice in those days, when people would just disappear and their family would never know what had happened. I was then transferred to another prison for political prisoners at Southerton, near Harare. Before they took me there they drove me to my flat, where they went through all my personal effects looking for any papers or evidence. While we were there I was allowed to change into a day dress but not shoes; I still had to walk in my bare feet.They did not find anything incriminating and marched me to their car. Everyone around the block of flats came out to watch me. Africans had that sorry look on their faces; the whites looked on with glee, as if to say: good, another guerrilla has been arrested. I was told not to talk to anyone whatsoever and not to discuss my case with uniformed police as it was now being dealt with by a CID special branch that dealt only with political prisoners.

In the meantime my brother-in-law and my nephew Charles and Juirus were still being held in the main prison as accomplices to my case. I have apologised to them, but I would like to apologise again in this book for what they went through because of having given me a roof over my head when I arrived in Zimbabwe. I shall always remain indebted to them for as long as I live. I was now in my new prison with a new name and when my family tried to look for the prison where I was being held they met with no success. I was in a cell where we slept on the floor, covering ourselves with dirty blankets full of lice. The toilet in the corner was just a hole in the floor with running water flushing night and day. There was no water to wash one's hands and one would use the toilet with everyone watching. There was a small window almost in the ceiling and the smell after someone had opened their bowels was something we just had to tolerate. In the next cell there were male political prisoners. The prison was near a main road; I could hear people shouting and laughing as they went or came from work, and the cars and buses out there. I used to amuse myself by looking for lice in my dress and hair and then killing them.

One evening a new policeman on night-duty came to count us for the night. As he looked at me he nearly fainted with shock, for he was looking at his aunt. He asked me why I was in there and I told him no one knew where I was being held, and that my name was Alice. At that prison all prisoners used to have the doors of the cells opened twice a day, and everyone would come out and sit in the fenced court yard at nine in the morning for breakfast and six in the evening for supper. Prisoners who had their families nearby would have food brought from home so that they would not have to eat the horrible prison food. When my nephew had seen me in prison he had gone to tell all my family where I was, but he told them not to say who had told them, for he would lose his job. The following morning there was so much food for breakfast that I had to give some to the others who had no food. My niece Priscilla, who lived nearby, made sure that there was breakfast and supper every day I was held in there, and some members of the family contributed towards the expense of the food. My mother contributed, and I want to thank my niece and her husband who contributed so much by letting people stay at their house and cooking the food which was being brought to me daily. I shall never forget their support during the time I was in prison.

I was at that time being taken for interrogations every morning to another prison, driven by an African policeman who would sometimes stop on the way to buy me a hot dog or a sausage roll and a bottle of Coca Cola. He would ask me to wipe my mouth so that no one would notice that I was being fed on the way. I would find two white men waiting for me; I still remember the name of the little white man, as he was called Tiny. On the Friday of the second week of my interrogation, as I was being led to the police car waiting to take me to the interrogation centre, I saw my mother with one of her grandchildren. She was dressed in her Salvation Army officer's uniform and looked so unhappy to see me being led away as a convict. She quickly ran across to the officer who was with me and started begging him to let her talk to me, and please to release me, because I had done nothing to warrant all this harassment. She insisted on coming with us as she wanted to see where they were taking me. The officer felt sorry for her, because he was a fellow African only doing what his masters asked him to do. He dropped them a few yards away from the centre and told them to wait until he took me back to the main prison. When I arrived I was asked to sit in the fenced area while they dealt with the case before mine. I was surprised to see my brother-in-law sitting opposite. We managed to talk to each other in such a way that the officers would not notice that we were talking. My brother-in-law said to me (looking on the floor and making drawings in the sand) that he thought we were going to be released that day, and that his son had already been released. I started making drawings as well, and asked him how he knew. He said that they had to release us for they had not found any evidence with which to convict us.

I was then called into the office where Tiny was with another tall white man. I was a smoker at that time and I was surprised when they offered me a cigarette. After a few seconds Tiny said I was going to go home, but they would like me to supply them with the names and addresses of the people who were fighting against them. If I did I would be given a nice house, and my children sent to the best schools in the country; but if I did not I could find myself in terrible trouble. They would hunt down my children wherever they were. I was now so angry that I stood up in that office and called their bluff. I told them that they were killers anyway, and were not going to threaten me through my children. If they wanted to kill me they could, but not my children. They looked at each other and the big white man said to Tiny: take her home. He said they would be watching me all the time. But I was not finished with them yet, for I wanted to know why I had been arrested, and why I was being released now. I had now lost earnings by being there and needed money to pay my rent and my son's school fees. Tiny said to me he would meet me in the Monomutapa Hotel lounge the following week and we would talk about it. They knew that I was right and that I was prepared to go all the way to fight for my rights.

I was taken home and on our way we picked up my mother and her grand-daughter. My brother-in-law had already been taken home. At home that day there was a wonderful get-together. We felt so dirty we used disinfectant to wash ourselves; I cut my hair and burnt the dress I had been wearing in prison. It was nice to feel clean and to wear underwear after two weeks of wearing nothing under one's dress. The prison smell remained for a long time, and I still had nightmares. Even today I sometimes shiver when I think of those horrible days I spent in prison for nothing I had done; nothing except being black and living in my own country.

The following week I kept my appointment with Mr Tiny. When I walked in there I stood near Tiny for five minutes, looking at him looking at his watch and thinking that I was late for the appointment. Then I said hello to him and he realised that I had been there for some time; he said that I looked different. I suppose he meant clean and well-dressed. He offered me a drink which I declined, for I just wanted to know what he had to say to me. I did not want to spend my time with him, for I was now feeling a hot hatred against the white regime. They had imprisoned me for nothing. I told Tiny that I hated the white Rhodesians before, but not as much as I hated them now. I knew I had nothing to lose, and I was soon going to help to dispose of them with my vote. Tiny began to repeat his threats, and I said he could go ahead with whatever he wanted to do, but I would make sure that he would not remain in the country if we won the majority rule. He just smiled as if to say it would never happen. He offered me some money, about two hundred dollars, which was nothing, but I needed money to pay my bills. After a few weeks I heard that Tiny had left for South Africa.

8

Divorce, and a Trip to New York

I now had to get on with my life and think of what I wanted to do to have a life of my own, to forget and put behind me all the bad things that had happened to me. I went back to work where the few Africans who worked there felt very sorry for me and welcomed me with a bottle of wine; but the white people did not speak to me for they still believed I was fighting a guerrilla war against them. I continued to work and at the same time I started divorce proceedings against Simon. By that time his girlfriend was expecting their child. On the day of our meeting at the court I was very much in control of myself and no longer in love with him. Even if he had come to ask for forgiveness I would not have taken him back. When I was in the court I looked across to where he was and I felt no flutter in my heart, but only contempt. I was quite astonished at how he looked. Although still smartly dressed he appeared to me now a very mean, selfish person. It did not take more than half an hour for our marriage to be dissolved, but I did not get anything from that marriage. I was only to be given £50 per month for our son who was living with me, until he was eighteen years of age. When I walked out of the court I felt drained. My sister phoned to enquire what had happened and how I felt. I told her that I felt nothing at all, and I was going out with my friends to celebrate. We did have a wonderful time, for I was free from loving him and free from a marriage that had made my life a living hell. Simon would come at the end of the month to my workplace to hand me the £50.00 cheque.

It took me a long time to start looking at men as people who are there for women, and who can be nice to their wives or girlfriends. My ambition was to see my three boys get an education. I did not want another dad in my children's lives.

I worked at the same company for a year, during which time the Rhodesia/Zimbabwe marriage had come to an end and the people of Zimbabwe had cast their vote in favour of the National Party, led by Robert Mugabe. I then went to see the new Minister of Home Affairs – the very same man who had given my children and me a roof over our heads the first time we arrived in London – Taurayi Ziyambi. He was pleased to see me and asked what I was doing and how my husband was. I told him what had happened since he last saw me in England and he told me about his family and that he was married to a West Indian lady who was a lawyer, as he was. I then asked him if there were any jobs going in his ministry. Because of my nursing background he asked me if I would work in the police medical stores, as the white person who was working there had left for South Africa. I thanked him, and the following month I began work in the police, as a medical stores officer.

Before I started, my sister and I decided to go for a holiday in America, but I had no money to pay for my flight. My sister on the other hand was a very rich woman. We wanted this holiday together because we were friends as well as sisters. We loved each other; she was my hero, although we would fight at times. I was never jealous of her money but very proud of her achievements, and to be known as her sister. We had a system in Zimbabwe whereby you could fly now and pay later; you had to be employed and paid a good salary, so I had no problems with that. We booked our flight to New York. I was going to stay with my son and my sister was to stay with her daughter. My sister was putting on a show of knitted dresses, blouses and skirts made by hand by women in Zimbabwe. The exhibition was being held in Manhattan. Arriving in New York, we went to her daughter's, and I phoned my son to come for me. When we arrived where he was staying I was shocked. I had thought he had a flat of his own, but he was occupying one of the rooms in a flat of a young Zimbabwean couple, so that he had to sleep in their lounge and I occupied his room. That was when I felt I should not have gone to New York as I realised that I had put my son in an embarrassing situation.

One day my sister invited me to meet her at her show in Manhattan; my son escorted me there and went back to work. I spent the whole day there and we had a lovely time. Towards evening my sister said it would be better if I started to go back to Brooklyn while it was still light. I went down into the subway; I was frightened but determined to reach where I was going. I thought since I had lived in London I would have no trouble with another underground railway system, but I was in for a shock. Every train seemed to be going down town. I travelled to and fro on the subway, trying to recognise where I had come from. I asked many people, black and white, but I could not understand their way of directing a stranger. I asked one elderly black woman who just looked at me and said to follow her, but then I became suspicious of her, so when she was going up the stairs I just turned back down to the bottom, then sat on a bench and started to cry, for I realised that I was lost. I did not know what to do; I could not go back to Manhattan where my sister was, for I did not know how to get there. My son had phoned my sister to ask her when I was going to be back. My sister informed him that I had left at six o'clock and it was now eleven at night. My son, panicking, called his friend to help him to look for me. Just at that time I called his place and was told he had left for the nearest subway. But the friend informed my son when he phoned back that I had called, and told him the name of the place where I was, and when I phoned again they directed me to their nearest station. I was now even more frightened; there were drunkards now wanting to sleep on the subway, as well as homeless people and thieves. When I got out of the train and looked around for the way home a young, big black woman asked me if I needed help. She was very kind and when I said I was lost she took me by the arm to a cab office and barked at them to take me home, without harassment, because if anything happened to me they would have her to deal with. The driver never said a word to me but deposited me at my son's door. When he saw me he nearly fainted with relief. From that day I never went to meet my sister alone, and my son never allowed me to go anywhere without him.

The time came for us to go back to Zimbabwe.I left a day before my sister, and arrived en route at Gatwick Airport at seven in the morning, with only five dollars, and thirteen hours to wait before my flight to Harare was to take off. I just sat there feeling hungrier and hungrier. When Zimbabwe Airways called for passengers to check in, I could not wait to be on the plane for then I knew I would have a meal. We took off but before we were given a meal we were given a complimentary half-bottle of champagne (Zimbabwe Airways used to do that). I drank mine so quickly on an empty stomach that I felt light-headed and fell asleep. I was later awakened for a meal so nice that I ate every morsel and went back to sleep until we touched down the next morning at Harare. I had no money left for a taxi as I had used the five dollars to buy a cup of coffee at Gatwick. So I phoned my brother in-law to come for me. I was glad to be home.

A few months later my son wanted to come home from America to work in Harare. When he came he got employment in the office of statistics. Although he was born in Zimbabwe he was a baby when we left Rhodesia for Zambia, where he was educated, and after high school he left for America. When my son started to work in Harare the situation was not as he thought it would be. For he could not speak the local language. The local people did not take this well; they thought he was showing off. After a few months we decided that he should go back to America, but the problem was to get money for his air fare. We then approached friends and relatives to act as guarantors. One friend agreed to be a guarantor but when we took the forms to his bank the application was refused. We were disappointed, but then we thought of Simon as a guarantor. My son was very direct with him, and though he wanted to refuse he persuaded him to sign the forms; the application was approved, and after a few days he flew back to America.

The block of flats where I was living was now being sold, so I had to move out and rent one room in my cousin's house. She was a very nice lady. We bought groceries and cooked our meals together in her kitchen. My younger son came with me and shared a large bedroom with my cousin's son, and they became good friends. My cousin and I were the same age. She later visited and stayed with me at my flat in England; we were friends as well as cousins. While I was staying in her house I started to think of coming back to England. My health was failing and I was finding the journey to and from work very tiring. I sold all my possessions and moved in with my elder sister, who gave me a type of cottage, that the white men's employees used to live in, but I was thankful to her for giving me a roof over my head. Her daughter used to sleep in the same room with me and even today I love her as if she was my daughter. When I was at work one day a lorry was driven to my sister's house and the driver asked for me. They had come to collect my possessions to pay for the outstanding bill for my son's flight to America. My sister showed them the few dresses I had and my single bed and said that if they wanted to take them they could. They told her that Simon had directed them there. Of course he had to pay the bill; after all he was not my son alone.

9

Nursing in London – Life as a Single Working Mum

I booked a flight to England, and went to stay with my nephew and his family in the north. The family was good to me and I had a wonderful time with them before I moved to London to work as an agency nurse. When I arrived in London from the north I booked myself into a bed-and-breakfast. I had some money from the sale of my possessions and after a week I moved to a room in Walthamstow. I could cook my meals and eat in the landlord's large kitchen. He was a widower and had drinking problems, but was not violent to his tenants. I was shocked when I moved in, for the whole house was cold, there was no central heating, no heaters in the rooms and in my room no curtains but an old fashioned water tank in the corner. When water was pouring in there would be so much noise that it was impossible to sleep. I was working with an agency as a night nurse for seven nights a week; it was very difficult to sleep with the daylight shining through the window, and also the cold. Each time I came back to the flat in the morning after work I felt so cold I put a blanket over the window to block out the daylight, but there was nothing I could do to stop the noise of water pouring into the tank. I would go to work tired and with bloodshot eyes, but I was determined to carry on because I wanted to make money as quickly as possible.

There was another room which was unoccupied, a better room, not that it was warm in there, but I wondered what it was for. I found out. Every day at one in the afternoon a man and a woman would come into that room and I could hear noises of these two people making love. I later asked the young man who occupied the other room and he confirmed my suspicions. That was another thing which would wake me up for they were a noisy pair.

I decided to buy a duvet and an electric blanket with my first pay. My landlord was not pleased as he thought I would be using more electricity, but he never confronted me. He used to open the tenants' rooms to see what they had. To make the situation worse, when he got drunk in the evening he would urinate and open his bowels in the kitchen because he would be too drunk to climb the stairs to the toilet. One day I went down to the kitchen in the evening to boil some water to have a wash before I went to work, and as I turned from the sink I put my foot in urine and excrement. When I looked down I could not believe what I was looking at. I was so angry I called him out of his room and confronted him. I told him that I was going to inform the Social Services about his behaviour. He looked scared and from that time the hygiene situation improved slightly.

There was no telephone in the house so the agency would ask me to phone them in the evening. I had to get up and walk to the post office, which was not near but, I had to do it for I needed work. I did this whether it was raining or snowing; I became a workaholic. I would go to the launderette to do my washing once a week. One day as I was going there singing a tune from the Salvation Army songbook, there was an older lady walking behind me on her way home. She said hello, and as I turned and looked at this lovely black woman, who looked my mother's age before she died, suddenly I began to cry. She took me in her arms and let me cry; then I told her my problems and she listened. From that day we used to meet in the high street, and I started calling her Mum, and she would introduce me as her adopted daughter. I had needed to cry for a long time.

After nine months living in the house in Walthamstow I needed better accommodation. The landlord realised that I was about to move out and one day when I came back from work in the morning I found my room with curtains on the window and a new carpet on the floor. I spoke to the young man who used to tell me what was going on in the house, and he told me that the landlord was thinking of asking me to go out with him, and that if I agreed the house would be mine. I felt low that he thought I was so desperate

I would go out with him for the sake of the house. From then on I was determined to move out as soon as I could. I was lucky to be introduced by a workmate to a lady from Kenya who had another large house in Walthamstow. I went to see the room; it was not large but there was a double bed, a television and it was very warm. I would take it and paid a deposit. The day I moved out I did not go to work, and after I had made myself comfortable I felt so tired. I had the most wonderful night, for I slept right through without any disturbances. I lived in this house for the next two years and I became very good friends with my landlady. We understood each other and gave each other space.

I decided I wanted to start dating. About this time I started going out with friends whenever I had a chance. I also decided to get a permanent job, as I was really tired of working for agencies. They would call any time if a hospital needed a nurse, and it made it impossible to go out or plan ahead. I applied for a job with a private hospital and I was lucky to be accepted. It was not so far from where I was living. When I went out with friends one night to a club I met a nice man of my age. I was not seriously dating but later I found out that he was serious, and we went out for about two years. He was a man who kept his promises. He showed me the best of London: good restaurants and good food, the best theatres in London. He had a good job as an architect. For our first Christmas he invited me to his company celebration party. An orchid spray was delivered to me before he came to pick me up for the party. He was perfect when it came to treating ladies in a proper manner, but he had the most boring jokes – he was a really stiff-upper-lip Englishman. I would find myself drained of strength trying to keep up with his ways; each time he brought me home from visiting friends or from a restaurant I used to sigh with relief knowing that I could be myself again. After two years it was proving to be too much for me.

When I had been renting from the landlady who had became a friend for a couple of years she advised me that I should buy my own house or flat. I thought about this seriously and decided to go for it. I bought a two-bedroomed flat with a kitchen, bathroom and a lounge. I liked it and it was situated in a good area. In the meantime I moved out of my rented flat to another one while work was being done in my own new flat, for it was cheaper and nearer for me to go and look at the work which was being done. In the flat there was a red deep-pile carpet on the stairs leading to the main bedroom; in the lounge there was a deep shag-pile carpet, the bathroom and kitchen were carpeted and the flat was central-heated. I went on my knees and cleaned the carpets, the bathroom and toilet until every corner of the flat was clean to my satisfaction. I then moved in, but there were no chairs to sit on. I had bought a new hob and a new double oven, a new refrigerator and a washing machine. Any friends who came to see me had to sit on the carpet. A few weeks later I hired a television – I needed that to keep myself sane by watching some programmes before I went to work. I had my telephone line and now I could speak to my children in America, Sweden and Zimbabwe. I could also get in touch with my sisters and friends in and outside England.

I asked my man friend to come and see my flat. When he came I could sense he was not pleased, and I wondered why. I came to the conclusion that he thought I was now better off than I was when I was renting, and I did not need him. I thought to myself maybe he was one of those men who did not like to see women doing well for themselves. He phoned me the next day to apologise for his behaviour and asked how I was going to manage paying the mortgage. Maybe he thought I would ask him to help me. I told him I would manage, and that he need not bother to contact me again, the relationship was finished. That was that; I never saw him again.

I was now working seven nights on at my private hospital and doing agency work for five out of the seven nights I was off from my hospital, so as to be able to pay the mortgage and other expenses. I carried on for almost three years and as the payments became less and easier, I began to cut down on the agency work. I thought life was now good for me; I was looking forward to doing much more for myself and my children. Although they were now adults still they were my boys and I wanted to give them everything. My eldest boy would tell me off and told me to look after myself. I would send money to the younger boy who was in Zimbabwe to fly him over to America, and his brother would do the same. My middle boy had come from Sweden and was staying with me while working as a chef.

It is during such times when one thinks life is not too bad that one is taken by surprise. One night I was preparing to go to work and my sister in Zimbabwe was trying to phone me. For some reason or other the call was not coming through. They contacted a friend of the family in London to go to my flat and let me know that my other sister had shot herself and was dead. I thought this person was pulling my leg, but he said he wished that it was a joke; my sister had been trying to phone me all afternoon. I was too shocked to cry, and could not think of my strong sister leaving her children and husband, not to mention all the wealth she had worked for. I phoned home and spoke to my other sisters, who could only say to me yes, she was dead. I started screaming on my own; I had no one to talk to. I just sat on the floor for the whole night. In the morning I phoned our embassy. I was still using the old British passport, and it had expired. I was told if I went out I would not be allowed to come back into the country. I phoned my sister again and spoke to other relatives, and they said I must just grieve on my own; my sister would not have wanted me to fly back home. I must mention here that but for my sister who was now dead I would not have been able to come back to England. She encouraged me for she knew that I was not doing so well in Zimbabwe after my divorce. We used to phone each other when I came back to England, and one time she came to see me on her way to America. She stayed in the Strand Hotel where I went to see her and slept there, chatting and laughing all night. On her way back to Zimbabwe she came to see me for the day; we went to the market and I bought her an electric breadcutter, not because she could not afford it, but I wanted to show my appreciation of all she had done for me. That was the last time I saw her before her death. It was difficult to grieve on my own. I would phone home just to be able to speak to my other sisters, then would feel worse afterwards because I could hear so many people's voices crying. I thank God that my mother had died two years before. My sister and her husband were rich people; they had worked very hard for their money and were now running businesses in Harare, so she was able to drive my mother to the doctor if she needed one, and was able to go and see her regularly where my mother was living in the rural area. She organised a water hole to be dug right beside our mother's house so she did not have to walk far to carry water.

I continued to work hard; there was no more going out. I was now 56 years old and I realised that I was getting old. I was aware that there were very few men who would want to go out with an old woman – most men, the older they were, the more they wanted to go out with a young woman. I must say I was lucky because I always looked much younger than my age. After a few years I contacted a friend who was going out with a man living in Brighton. She was also Zimbabwean and a divorcee; a very beautiful woman. I wanted to talk to her about the problem of being alone. I was beginning to be frightened of growing old on my own. We talked on the phone for a long time and she understood what I was going through. She also told me she was going to get married. When the time of her marriage was near she asked me to give her away, so on that day I travelled to Brighton, a place I had never been. It was a good wedding, and we enjoyed ourselves. After the reception I left for London and went back to work. My niece was now living with me and studying baking technology at the University, so I was not so lonely. I had someone to talk to; we had a lovely time together. She was like my own daughter, and still is. My friend who was now married came to see me one day and brought with her a newspaper cutting which advertised men and women for dates. She said I should try to write to any man who advertised for a soulmate. When she had gone I looked through this cutting she had brought me. I felt excited by this venture so I marked the one I thought sounded nice and started writing soon after I had got home from work. I had had my breakfast and now sitting in my bed I wrote with all my heart. During that time I felt my heart beating so fast that I was quite amazed. On my way to work that night I posted the letter and forced myself to forget all about it. In my heart I thought it did not matter if I did not hear from this man. I was not looking for someone with a lot of money; what I wanted was to love someone who could love me, even if he lived in a council flat. I needed a friend and a husband. I was never a person to remain single.

BOOK TWO

WILLIAM

10

How I Met the Man who Changed My Life

One morning I came back from work, had a bath as soon as I got home, then prepared my breakfast which I always took to my bedroom and ate sitting in bed and watching the morning programmes on the television. The telephone rang and I said hello with a tired voice. The person on the other end asked for my name and I said it was I speaking. Then he said he had received a letter from me. I became nervous; he sounded unsure and nervous as well. I said, yes, I did write, making my voice lighter and happier because he seemed to be lost for words. As he told me, it was the first time he had done such a thing, so I thought I would have to take control here, as men are easily frightened. Yet I did not want to overdo it in case I frightened him even more. We talked about our interests, and I asked him his name and surname. After our talk he said he would phone me the next day after work and wanted to know what time I came home in the morning. I was excited – and I was now 57 years old. The next day could not arrive soon enough. I wanted to go home and wait for this call. If he did not call then I would know that he was not interested, but the call came. I was now thinking I would have to meet this man. What did he look like? Was he bald-headed, old and walking with the aid of a stick, and driving a little old Morris car? But, I thought to myself, I did not care as long as we liked each other. I never thought of dating young men; I used to be horrified to see an older woman with a young man. We made arrangements to meet. I decided that I would go to where he lived, in Hove. Although I had been to Brighton I had travelled by car with friends, but now I was going to go by train. I worked my seven nights and was about to have the seven nights off. I told him I would travel on Tuesday and arranged the time we were going to meet at Hove Station, East Sussex. This was going to be a challenge and in my heart I was apprehensive, if not frightened. I informed my nieces that I was going to Hove for a blind date. They were not amused, and wanted the telephone number, the name and the address of the person I was going to meet in case I did not come back.

I woke up on that Tuesday morning determined to meet my destiny. I had a long bath and wore a pale blue suit; the skirt was a mini just above my knees. I bought a return ticket at Victoria Station for my train to Hove. I bought a newspaper to read on the train, but did not read it for I was clutching it too tightly in my hands, while in my heart and mind there were so many questions churning around. I was sweating with anticipation; I thought that if I did not find him waiting for me I would just turn round and get the next train back to London. When I arrived at Hove Station I was the only black woman there and I knew he could not miss me. He would be the one to come to me so I looked where the cars were parked. I did not see an old Morris car, and the man who was looking at me and pointing his finger at me, so I could confirm that I was the lady he was waiting for – this man did not look 70 years old, and as I looked at him I thought that he must be younger than me. He extended his hand to greet me and led me to his car, which was new, and Japanese. I was assisted into the car, and I thought to myself that all my assumptions so far were wrong. He was not bald; he had a full head of curly gold-blond hair. As we drove away from the station he asked me if I would like a cup of tea, and I said yes, please, so he drove to his house. We stopped in front of two houses which looked alike with black wrought-iron gates, a garage and a profusion of flowers (it was at the end of summer).

In the house he made tea for us and we could not stop talking. He wanted to know more about me and I wanted to know more about him. At about six in the evening we went to have dinner at an Indian restaurant. We talked all the way through the dinner; we did not eat all our food. He was listening and laughing most of the time, listening to what I was saying while I was being careful not to bore him. There was so much to say to each other that we did not realise how time was flying by; I was to go back to London that same day. He told me some of his life; how as a young man after the war in Germany he dated a young German woman and later married her. They had a baby girl, and divorced after twenty-five years. He then met another lady who was a receptionist at Seeboard where he, William, was a foreman. They married, but unfortunately she died of cancer after twenty years together, and there were no children between them. Neither of us wanted to say a lot about ourselves at our first meeting. After our dinner I said I had to go back to London as I was to be on duty the following night. He said he would take me to the station as soon as we finished our dinner. I was expecting him to ask me to go first to his house for coffee, as a woman I wanted to feel that he had been impressed by me and would want to have more time with me. I was pleased with his name, William John Trewin; he said friends called him Bill, but I wanted to call him William. He took me to the station and stayed with me for some time, then he gave me a kiss on the cheek, and I had to be content with that. On the train to London I did not think I had impressed him. I liked him but I did not know if he liked me.

When I got back to my flat, my niece was waiting up for me, for she was worried that I had gone to meet a stranger. She wanted to know all about this man but, I begged her to let me sit down first and have a cup of tea. I have never had a cup of tea brought to me so fast. Then I told her everything. She asked me if I liked him and I said yes I did, but I did not know if he liked me. I decided to phone him to let him know that I had arrived and to thank him for the lovely dinner. We talked for a while and he said he would phone me the next day at eleven in the morning after my night duty. I went to work wondering if he was going to phone as promised. I became so nervous that my colleagues at work noticed that my mind was elsewhere, and after my duty in the morning I made sure I was at home before time so that there could be no excuse for missing the call. At eleven the call came. My heart was beating so fast. We talked for some time and he said he would phone me when I woke up at six in the evening, before I went to work. From then on he phoned twice a day.

11

Courtship at Fifty-Seven

I used to work seven nights on then seven nights off, but now I was going to Hove for five days to be with William. He told me later that he had been apprehensive about making love to me, as he had heard that it took a real man to make love to a black woman and satisfy her; and I was also thinking that a white man was not so much of a man as a black man. We were both wrong as we found out later. We dated for three or four months and during that time my life changed: I was happy and I had life in front of me. My friends at work were surprised by the change in me. We would drive around East and West Sussex; William would take me shopping in Chichester, Eastbourne, Worthing, Tunbridge Wells and the local shops in Brighton. I was thoroughly enjoying myself; I could choose what I wanted, and it was there that we noticed people looking at us and I suppose they were surprised to see these two mature people of different colours walking hand in hand. William noticed this and each time someone stared he would put his arm around me and kiss me. I felt safe because he did not care and so I did not care either. He would buy me expensive clothes, shoes and handbags; I felt very spoilt and I loved it. He treated me like a woman, I remember every time we went to buy a pair of shoes he would kneel down to remove the shoes I was wearing and help me to try on the new ones. The sales ladies would look on with surprise and some would comment, saying there were not many men left to give women such respect.

We decided to go away, to be on our own to be together. I had been alone for a long time and this was going to be a challenge.

William had been alone for almost eighteen months after his wife died, so both of us were going to have to learn to be with someone all the time. I had been off work for a few weeks. I had hurt my back lifting a patient, and had been to see a consultant because I was having problems walking. After the investigations and X-rays I was advised to take a month off work, so that helped to decide us to go on holiday together. We decided to go to Jersey and Guernsey for two weeks. This would be my first holiday for a long time, as I had not been able to afford one, with a mortgage to pay plus other expenses. I was excited to think that at long last I was to fly again. Although we were not going abroad it was still the best thing that had happened to me for a long time. William sent me a cheque for £800 to book the holiday. I was to find out later that I could choose anywhere I liked to go on holiday, and he would agree with me. I booked to fly first to Jersey, then Guernsey. I booked as a married couple, and of course I had asked his permission to use his name for it would be easier in the hotels. When the time came for us to fly out his daughter and her husband drove us to Gatwick Airport. Although William had told them that he was dating me, we had not met, and that was as good time as any to meet each other. They were very nice and had known beforehand I was black. His daughter gave us her blessing. William told me later that his son-in-law thought I was too young for him, and that he was a cradle snatcher. I thought that was very funny – I was 57 years old.

When we arrived at Jersey Airport I heard our name being called for the car which had been sent for us by the hotel. I felt warm within myself, although we were not married. I thought that at least I was being called a Mrs with a man beside me, while for so long I had been called a Mrs without the man I had been married to. We were taken to our hotel, one of the best in Jersey and a five-star hotel. It was beautiful and the food was superb. Guests and employees in the hotel would stare, but we did not care. After a few days we won the waiters round, because we would talk to them, and wherever we sat there was laughter. We were in a world of our own; we were there to know each other and enjoy ourselves. We hired a car to take us wherever we wanted to go. We drove around and went shopping and one day ended up walking into a large jewellery store. I went around, looking not thinking of buying anything. William was by my side as I was looking at the engagement rings. They were so beautiful, and he suddenly asked me over my shoulder: which one did I like? I said to him why? He then said: should we get engaged? I said yes, my heart beating fast with excitement. I kept looking at the opal ring, which was quite expensive, but he could see that I liked it. The sales lady came and showed it to me, and I tried it and it looked very nice. William said I could have it, I was so happy the sales lady ordered a bottle of champagne to be opened, so we had a drink at eleven thirty in the morning, and of course I was already drunk with happiness. We bought some earrings and a gold chain and drove off to another store which sold pearl necklaces and earrings. Here we met antagonism. They did not want to attend to us, and would not look at me. I suppose they thought that a white man with a black woman has no money to buy pearls. As William lifted a necklace and tried it on me I could see the sales lady making a beeline towards us. William was now playing them at their own game. He went and looked at some earrings; by this time two sales ladies were now talking to us and calling us sir and madam. We chose a necklace and two pairs of earrings, and when he took out wads of £50 and £100 notes the sales ladies' eyes nearly popped out, and they couldn't do enough for us. We laughed about the mentality of people who look down on others just because of their colour, dress and accent; for one never knows what they have in their wallets.

We stayed in Jersey for 6 days and on the 7th day we flew to Guernsey. I liked Guernsey; the hotel was new and very nice. On our first day there, after we had been shown to our room, we went to the restaurant to have tea and something to eat. We sat there while a man played music on the piano; we sat for some time waiting for a waiter to come and take our order. They would look at us as if we were not supposed to be there. The next day when we went back the waiters had thawed slightly towards us, so after our meal they were given a good tip. From that day everyone was so nice to us. Our relationship was taking shape; we were comfortable with each other and enjoying each other's company. We would go swimming every day. William likes swimming. I was not a good swimmer, but he taught me; and I enjoyed the sauna,

Jacuzzi and Finnish baths. We stayed for 4 days in Guernsey and left on the 5th day of our stay.

When we flew back to Gatwick from Guernsey, we held hands all the way and we still do today, especially when we are flying, for he gives me a sense of warmth and protection. We went to my place in Leyton, London, to show him my flat. My nieces were waiting for me; they wanted to see this man who had stolen my heart. They were not disappointed. They liked him, and William was comfortable with them. The next day he spent doing DIY in my lounge; putting shelves up for my books and buying dried flowers to decorate the lounge. After two days with me he left for Brighton. William never could stand London. When he left, I felt alone. I did not want him to leave, although I did not show it. I had to go to work, and he went away with the promise that I would see him after seven days when I would be off. It was now the pattern of my life to be with William when I was off-duty. When I returned to work I told my friends about my engagement, although it was not official yet. They were pleased for me and congratulated me.

I had met William in September 1994 and the following year in March I was on my usual visit to Brighton when he said he had arranged a dinner with his daughter and her family. I said that was nice, but in my heart I was apprehensive for I had not met the children yet; a boy of 19, a girl of 16 and another girl of 9 years old. I need not have worried for they were the most wonderful family. We drove from our house and met them, then went together in three cars to a restaurant. We sat at our reserved table; William's daughter sat between her father and myself. After ordering our meal, talking and laughing, William said to everyone that there was a reason why he had wanted to have dinner with the family. Then he looked at me and asked to marry him. He apologised for being unable to go down on his knee, because of his daughter who sat between us. Everyone laughed, but immediately went quiet, waiting for my answer. It was Valentine's Day. I looked at everyone at the table and then at William and said a loud yes. We toasted each other, and it was the most wonderful time in my life, for now I had someone to love and someone who loves me. I realised that I would never be afraid of life, that I would always have someone by my side. I had been afraid to be ill when I was alone. It was the most beautiful thing that had ever happened to me for a long time.

Our relationship became solid from then on and we started to talk about a wedding. I told my nieces who were delirious with happiness; I now had to tell my sons about my impending marriage. I wrote to my eldest son although I could have phoned, but I thought that it would be better if I wrote to him. I said I was going to get married to a white man. He later phoned me and we had a good talk. I told him that I loved them all very much and that I would not change my sons for anything, but I needed companionship and that now I would never be alone again. He asked me if I loved him. I said I did and I knew he loved me. He then asked if I was sure that I would be happy with a white man. I said that so far I did not see him as a white man but a man I loved, so he said that he was pleased for me and wished me the best of luck. My other two sons were pleased that I had found someone to share my life with. I could understand my eldest son's doubts. He was concerned for me, as he had seen some black girls in America who had suffered at the hands of their white husbands.

William and I decided that we were going to be married in April. I had to give notice at my work in London and also go to the registry office of my borough in Walthamstow for the banns to be put up, and have invitation cards printed. I had to shop for my wedding dress and decide what kind of flowers I wanted; we had to find a place where the reception was going to be held and I had to see to the wedding cake; but William solved this, for near his home there was a lady who made wedding cakes. She also arranged with her friend to supply flowers.

Time was flying by fast but I was feeling wonderful within myself. I had had a white wedding before when I was young, but, this was going to be different, for I knew what I wanted and money was no problem. It was going to be William's first white wedding; his previous marriages were at the registry office. We decided that the reception would be held in a public house near our home; the upper floor was booked, and disco music was hired to play at our wedding. I then decided to get in touch with the Salvation Army officer at the nearby Salvation Army Citadel in Brighton, for I felt that although it was my second and William's third marriage, I wanted our marriage to be blessed by a church minister. I phoned the major to asked him if he could bless our marriage at the venue where the reception was being held. He said he saw no reason why not and could he come to our house to talk to us through the wedding arrangements? We were happy to welcome him and he was a jovial man, very free to talk to. I then told him all about my life from when I was young growing up as the daughter of a Salvation Army officer, going to Salvation school and getting married to my first husband in the Salvation Army. Now I was asking him to give us a blessing at our wedding. I was apprehensive that he might refuse to come because of the reception being held in a pub, as Salvationists are not supposed to drink alcohol; but he did not mind. When he was about to go after our lengthy talk, William suddenly said to him that he was sure he had met him before, and the major said he thought he had been to this house before. He then remembered that he had been in this house to pray when William's second wife had died, and went on to say that God works in a miraculous way. I was amazed that he had come to this house twice, first in a time of grief and then in happy circumstances. William's late wife was not a Salvationist, but she had seen and heard their music in open air meetings in Brighton and she said to William that she would like the Salvation Army to come and sing for her if she died. William kept that promise and when his wife died he went to the Salvation Army to ask if they could come to his house to sing at his wife's funeral. William has never forgotten the sermon, which was delivered by the same officer who was going to bless our wedding.

The wedding day was drawing near, I had given my notice at my hospital and I think almost everyone was really happy for me. I had put my flat up for rent and two men were going to move in the day I was to move out. I needed the money to keep up with the mortgage, although I was still going to go to work after my marriage, in Brighton or any other towns nearby. William was going to hire a van to drive to London to collect all my belongings. He arrived in the afternoon and I left him there to go to work for the last night, with my niece to help him pack my belongings in the van. In the morning when I came back from work they had finished packing, and it was time for me to have a bath and leave.

William and I left and arrived in Brighton at sunset, we went into the house; he made us a cup of tea and I just burst into tears, I was confused, thinking that I had now moved form my own place, and was now here under someone else's roof. So many questions started buzzing in my head; only one thing kept me sane – that I loved this man and was going to marry him. He looked at me when I was crying and said I was going to be all right, it was natural that I should feel that way. The next morning we started putting things straight. Most of my belongings went into the storeroom because the house did not need any more furniture. We went to the registry office to book the date of our marriage. After that it was just a matter of waiting for the big day, which was going to be on the 8th April, 1995.

12

The Wedding

On the night before our wedding William went to stay with his daughter and family. I had my nieces and friends at his house for a hen night. William's daughter was there; she was going to drive me to the registry office and be a witness to her father's marriage. Her son was to be best man to his grandfather. On my side my niece was going to be the maid of honour and witness to my marriage. My colleagues from London had hired a bus to come to my wedding, and I was very proud and touched. When the hen night finished and everybody had gone to sleep my niece and I spent the rest of the night talking about the excitement of the following day. We were to be at the registry office in the morning at 11 o'clock. William was there and we went inside; I went to sit down with my niece and my nephew who was to give me away. Then I saw William coming to me asking for the paper from the London registry office, stating that banns had been put up and I was free to marry. I had only a receipt; I never knew I had to collect a paper stating that I could marry. Brighton registrar insisted on having the right piece of paper, in black and white, or there would be no wedding conducted. We were all devastated – there was to be no wedding held that day. I had wasted people's time; and the food would all be wasted. Then we thought of the Salvation Army officer who was there. William asked him if he could marry us in the name of God; and we would see about the registry office the following week. He agreed, so we asked all our guests to go to the pub where we were to have our reception. We would have our wedding conducted there, and then the reception.

We said our promises to each other there, and I did not care about the registrar who was an old stick who only did things by the book. We had a lovely time, people danced and drank and forgot all about the fiasco of the morning. We thanked the major and he left.

The following Monday we went to London to collect my papers as we were still going to be married at the registry office; the officer there gave me my papers and apologised for not telling me that I should have collected the papers before I left for Brighton. We drove back to Brighton and next day we went to book our marriage. We had to inform my niece and William's daughter to come on that day to witness the marriage. We had to go all through the marriage vows we had gone through at the pub, whether we liked it or not, otherwise we would not be considered married. After that we all went and had a lovely lunch at a restaurant. Our guests left and now we were surely married. Since then we have celebrated our wedding anniversary on both dates or sometimes we just choose the date when we are free; but both dates are very important to us.

We did not go away for a honeymoon. We waited for a year as we wanted to go to Zimbabwe to show my husband my country and my relations. I wanted to start work in Brighton and establish myself in a job and then request a holiday. I did not go to work immediately. I stayed home for six weeks. I wanted to know my new home and for us to get to know each other, to find out my new husband's likes and dislikes in things such as food. I was lucky in that William could eat almost everything I cooked, and he loved spiced foods. Later I introduced him to our staple food, which is called sadza, and he loved it. I was really enjoying being at home and pampered, William would bring me a cup of tea in bed in the morning and to me that was luxury. After breakfast we would drive around West or East Sussex. Most times we would have a drink or food at a restaurant or a pub. We were doing whatever took our fancy. When the time came for me to go to work, William would cook if I were working a late duty, then we would eat together. He said since he was retired he would do all the work at home, that is ironing and all the housework, as well as the garden. William did not want me to work nights, he had told me that I did not have to work if I did not feel like it as we could live comfortably without me working, but I wanted to go to work. I was used to working and I would be bored just sitting at home. Besides it was nice to give each other space. We agreed on that and I was working 24 hours a week, which was just enough for both of us. I was now driving myself to work and my life was just wonderful.

One day my eldest son phoned from New York informing us that he was flying to Harare, arriving at Heathrow at 7a.m. and leaving for Harare at 8 p.m. and would like to visit us for a few hours. We went to meet him, and that was the first time that William met one of my sons. It was the foundation of a great friendship between them. I was very pleased with the outcome. My son was travelling with a friend who was also going to Zimbabwe to visit his parents; they both came to our house in Hove. Because it was summer the garden was a riot of colours and flowers, and the two young men were impressed. I took my son to show him our house and he loved it. He then said to me he really liked my husband and that I had at last found a soulmate and he was sorry that he had doubted my choice. I said to him he had only been concerned about my welfare and there was nothing to be sorry for. We later took them for lunch: they both wanted British fish and chips, as it was not the same in America. After that we took them back to Heathrow Airport for their flight to Harare. From then on my son came to visit us once a year. He liked to be with us and we liked to have him. William and my son would always talk to each other for a long time and still do so today. My other two sons also loved William and that made my happiness fulfilled.

The year after our marriage we flew to Harare to see my sisters and other relations. When we arrived at Harare Airport after ten hours' flight every one of my relations was there to welcome us. I was handed a bouquet of flowers from my sisters. We had hired a car before we left Britain and it was there for us; my sister's son who was on leave became our driver so everything was going according to plan. It was lovely to be home after eleven years, and with my new husband. I really missed my mother who had died a few years earlier. I thought she would have been pleased for me, because she was devastated when my first marriage broke down, and she did not want me to be alone without a husband. William was so easy with everyone that although some could not speak

English and he could not speak our language, they would try to speak to him with the little English they could master. We were invited to different houses for meals and barbecues; we enjoyed ourselves so much that time seemed to be flying by. We visited Victoria Falls, flying over by helicopter, and saw a rainbow over the falls. We cruised on the Zambezi River drinking champagne which the crew had opened to welcome my husband to the fold. That is the true acceptance of Zimbabweans to foreigners who are married to one of their own. William was touched with this kind of welcome and he really enjoyed himself. We then travelled by coach back to Bulawayo, where my eldest son who had arrived from America and my nephew were going to meet us in our hired car, and drive us to Harare. We arrived in Bulawayo and after waiting for them at the place we had arranged to meet we decided to book into a hotel. We had left a message at my brother-in-law's surgery where we knew they would call. The hotel was not a clean place to stay; we tried to get a drink but could not change our sterling. Their behaviour was arrogant and I wanted to have a go at them, but William was against it, so we went and sat in our room. After a short time the phone rang; my nephew and my son were downstairs. They were shocked to find us in such circumstances and immediately said we should leave, although it was about seven in the evening and quite dark and we were to drive to Harare, which was about two to three hundred miles away. They were adamant that we could not stay there for the night and told us that visitors had been robbed at night in that hotel. We were feeling hungry by now so we decided that we would have a meal halfway to Harare. We stopped in Gweru and the four of us enjoyed a wonderful meal. After that we continued on our journey though by now it was very dark. The two young men helped each other to drive and we arrived in Harare after midnight. My sister and her husband were delighted to see us, and we settled down for the night, tired but at home.

Time was now going towards the date of our departure to Britain. I had to visit my late sister's grave and those of other relations who had died during my absence. It was sad to see my sister's grave, a sister who was so strong during her lifetime and who had everything going for her. I have sometimes thought that if I had been in

Zimbabwe maybe she would have told me what was worrying her.

When our day of departure came, some cousins, nephews and nieces gave us gifts to take back to Britain. It was sad to leave my sisters and the good time we had had and we invited them to come and visit us.

We carried on with our lives when we got back to Britain. I went back to work, but my back was giving me problems, and I had to go into hospital for a laminectomy. It was a straightforward operation and from then on I have not had any problems.

13

William's Story

During the evenings when we used to talk about our lives William would tell me some interesting episodes from when he was young. I found out that he had gone through thick and thin to be where he was today. When I asked for his permission to write about his life as I had written about mine, he gave me his consent.

William was born on the 14th June 1924 to William John Trewin, senior, and his wife Kate. William John senior was born in Devon. His father left his mother, went to sea and never came back. He went to America and never got in touch with his family. The wife moved to Brighton and looked after her two boys and although she remarried she had no other children. When William senior was 19 years old he met Kate, the 17-year-old girl who was going to be his wife. After going out with him she became pregnant. Her parents were very upset and angry for to them she was a young girl and they did not trust this young man who had put their daughter in the family way. Kate loved her man and they got married. Kate had a son, then a girl who died in her infancy, then William John junior, my husband, followed by two sisters. There was only a one-year difference between all the children. When William was 3 years old his parents decided to go to Plymouth to find work, but there was no work to be found there. They then walked back to Brighton, a very exhausting journey for such young children, and without enough food to share between them. When they reached Brighton they went to the council who gave them a tent to live in temporarily until a house could be found for them. The tent was put up on the Brighton Race Hill. They were promised a house in the new housing estate which was being built. When the time came for them to move into their new home they were the first family there to have electricity in the house and running cold and hot water as well as an inside toilet and a bath. William's father was proud of his new house and would talk to his friends, who were still living in candlelit houses, about his wonderful house.

When William was 5 years old his mother became very ill with tuberculosis, of which she subsequently died. When she was in hospital children were not allowed to go in the wards; only husbands were allowed to go in on Wednesday and Sunday afternoons. Fortunately her bed was by the window, so she was able to turn and wave to her small children; ill as she was, she was able to smile and wave. After his mother's death his father was devastated and could not cope with such young children. His eldest child was 7, William was 5 and the girls were 4 and 2 years old. William's father married within 6 months of his wife's death. This never pleased Kate's family, though the children were too young to grasp the situation. Their stepmother was never cruel to the children, but life was never going to be the same again. Kate died when she was only 25 years old. The children grew up with their new mother and began to look after themselves. William grew up faster mentally. He was small in body, but strong, though never violent. He respected the lady who had replaced his mother, would do what his father asked and was always honest. When he was 7 years old his father would wake him up at five thirty in the morning to walk for three miles to the bakery to buy cheap stale bread, for fresh bread was more expensive. In a way he was his father's boy, although the father was a man who never showed any love to his children. At this time the stepmother had given birth to a daughter, who naturally needed more attention, but she remained a mother to her husband's children, making sure that they were fed and clean. When William was 12 years old his father sent him to a lady who made bread-and-butter pudding. William could not find the address and when he went back without the pudding his father beat him on his legs. He was covered in bruises for days. His father was a temperamental man at the best of times; one day he even threw a plate at his young daughter. Fortunately she was just bending to pick up her baby step sister and it just missed her. Another time William came home from playing with his friends and reported to his father that he had been beaten up by a policeman's son who was twice his size. His father told his older son to go with his brother and help him fight this other boy, but when they got there the older brother did not want to fight. He was no stronger than William and stood by looking at his brother being beaten up. There was nothing William could do, no one to feel sorry for him, so he just had to lick his wounds until he got better. During William's schooldays his father lost his job and was so short of money that William went to school without shoes. He had to buy old shoes from other children for his father could not afford to buy him a new pair of shoes.

At the age of 13 he started a Saturday job delivering groceries on a bicycle. Because William was small and the bicycle big he would would cycle sideways, and managed quite well. His pay was 2 shillings, and his father would demand 1 shilling and sixpence, leaving William with only a sixpence. At school William had a good voice and could sing very well. One day there was a singing competition at his school and he won first prize. He was given a silver cup which at this moment decorates our bookshelf. After leaving school at 14 he was now delivering bread as a full-time job for 11 shillings a week. His father got 10 shillings leaving him with 1 shilling. Having no mother at home who could stand up to his father, there was nothing he could do but to hand over the money. He worked at this job for one year, till a grocer near his home who had watched him going to and from work wearing a tie and collar and looking very smart called him over and offered him a job, because he appeared a trustworthy and a hardworking young man. He was to deliver groceries that had been ordered. As he was telling me this he suddenly said that it was the only job he had been sacked from. He used to collect the money from delivering the groceries, then go home for dinner. When he got home he would remove the apron, which had a pocket containing the money, while he ate. He reckons his father took five shillings from the pocket. When he got to work five shillings were missing. He thought he must have dropped them somewhere, but the same thing happened again the following week, and the third week, only a shilling at a time. The grocer accused him of stealing the money; William asked him to call the police because he was sure he was not stealing, but he was sacked instantly. The grocer's wife begged her husband to keep him but he would not hear of it. Two years later the grocer and his business were bombed (it was during the Second World War). He was killed, but the wife survived. Maybe if William had still been working for him he would have been killed as well.

William got another job after he was sacked, still delivering groceries. He worked at it for one year but left after he had been asked by his employer to do a job which was usually done by older men. When he refused he was told that whether he was told to scrub floors or clean toilets he must just do it – after all he was only an employee. William walked out and went to look for another job. This time he went to work for the Co-operative Dairy delivering milk with a horse and cart. At 17 years old he was still small but strong and he could control his horse well. People used to be amazed that such a small person could control so large a horse. He would get up at five in the morning to deliver the milk. During winter he would feel very cold because he did not have enough clothes on. One day he left his books at home. He rushed back on his horse and when he got home, called to his father to come outside and look after the horse while he collected his books. As his father was holding the tether he was pulled towards the door as the horse was following his master. William had to run back to calm the horse before his father was pulled through the door into the house. His father was very upset but to the children it was something to laugh about, though not in their father's presence.

William worked at the Co-operative Dairy for one and a half years during the Second World War, but once he was 18 he was called up to join the army. When William joined the army, he was sent for training at Aldershot army camp. After he had completed his training he was sent to Omagh in Northern Ireland, then posted to the border of Denmark and Germany as a gunner for one year. Soldiers would go into Germany to socialise when they were off duty and during that time William met the German girl who was going to be his wife. By this time William's father had lost his second wife and had remarried. They had a baby son whom he called William John. William never forgave his father for giving his name to another son. To him it showed that he no longer cared about him. This caused such a rift between the half-brothers that they have remained indifferent to each other to this day. When he was still in the army he used to see other soldiers receiving letters and parcels from their mothers and fathers, but he never did for he had no mother at home, and what new woman in a man's life would think of sending a present let alone writing a letter to a grown-up stepson? It used to make him feel sad to realise that there was no one at home who would think of him and that he would have to look after himself. His sisters at home were working hard to look after themselves, and it was war time and that made them drift apart. His relationship with the German girl was so good that they decided to get married. When the time came for him to leave for England he had to leave his new wife back in Germany, for she had to apply for the right papers to be allowed to come to Britain. He had no qualifications other than having been in the army, and he had to work to provide for his wife. When he returned he went to stay with his father who was now working for the Sussex Electricity Board as a repairer of stoves, and digging trenches to lay electricity cables, William went to look for employment at the same company and was offered a job on the roads digging trenches like his father. After a week his hands were bleeding and the skin from his palms was peeling off but he kept on and his hands after a while became hardened. He was paid £4.5.0d per week.

William had written a letter to the War Office to complain about the delay in his wife's joining him in Britain, and got himself into trouble because he had not done it through the proper channels. His wife was now in a camp awaiting her departure to Britain. When later she arrived they had to live with his father and his third wife. It was not a good situation for two women to share a kitchen and live under the same roof. William's wife was learning to speak English, and being German she was not appreciated – at that time most people did not like Germans because of the war. William would give his father money for rent and the rest of his money to his wife for her to look after, but when his father found out that he was giving his wife more money than him he confronted his son and they had a row. William and his wife decided that it was time to move out. They moved to several places before they found a place they thought was nice. His father was still unhappy about losing the money his son had been giving him, and decided to pay him a visit with his elder son to fight him. William ran into a nearby public house; the stepmother followed him inside but was thrown out by the owner. The next morning William went to his brother's house to confront him. His brother was never a fighter and not as strong as William, and refused to come out of his house, so William left and went to work. Since he was working at the same place as his father he knew that he would meet him there. He met him in the passage, cornered him and was going to beat him, but his father pleaded with his son not to fight but to shake hands and be friends. Other people who were passing by also pleaded with the young man not beat his father. He let go but refused to shake hands, and although they continued to work at the same place they remained almost strangers. They would only talk to each other if necessary.

William was now being recognised for his hard work but his father decided to leave his job at that time. William and his wife moved to another house, which was to be their permanent home, in Hove, Highdown Road (which is our home today). When they moved they had no money to buy a bed, and there were two rooms being rented unfurnished, a kitchen with a stove and a bathroom and a toilet. William went to ask for a loan from the grocer nearby and was given a loan of £12 to pay him back at £2 per week out of his wages of £5 a week. The rent for their room was £1.10d; there were no curtains and no other furniture. However these were luxuries they had to do without. The rooms were large; one room was going to be a bedroom and the other a dining room. William managed to buy a bed out of the loan and they began to settle in their new home, buying other furniture and curtains as time went by. Two years after they moved they had a baby girl who, though it had taken her a long time to arrive when she was born made William so happy that she was worth waiting for. She would be the only child they would have.

At work the management was laying off people and making them redundant, the foreman going round the sites where the men were working and stopping and pointing at men who were digging trenches. This would mean that their work was finished and that they were no longer needed. This action caused a lot of stress among the workers for they did not know what would happen to them each day they went to work. One day the foreman drove his van by where William was digging and stopped there, watching him for a long time. William kept on digging as if he was not aware of the man's presence. After a time he drove off leaving William sweating, for he could not imagine what he would have done if he had been made redundant, but he knew that he was a good worker and that there was very little reason why he would be laid off work. He was a man who would go to work even when he was not feeling well and work overtime if he could, for he wanted his wife to have nice things which they could afford only by working hard.

A few years later a friend asked him if he wanted to make extra money working for the Territorial Army driving huge lorries delivering army goods to different depots. He agreed and he worked for the army for one year during which time he was thinking of resigning from his main job. Then the same foreman who he thought was going to make him redundant called William to his office to ask him if he wanted to work on the tools, that is, to learn how to be an electrical cable jointer. It was a breakthrough for him; in a way it was a promotion. After 16 years working as a jointer he was promoted to be a foreman; his family was pleased for at last there would be a bit more money. He now had a company van and a telephone at home so that he could be contacted at any time of day or night if he was needed. Although he was pleased with the promotion he was apprehensive, for he had never been good at spelling, in fact this knowledge was non-existent, so he commenced teaching himself. He bought a dictionary and exercise books, and would listen to people at work and note how they spoke and used words. When he got home he would look them up in the dictionary. This was done every evening without fail. Still today he writes in his diaries every evening. Sometimes if I forget what I did last month on a certain day he always refers to his diaries. He now has piles of these diaries containing events which happened years ago, and I hope one day I will read them. He used to have rows with his wife during this time as she wanted to go out, understandably as she was young but he wanted to work so that they could pay for the things they wanted to buy. He never wanted to get things on credit or borrow money for going to the pub or to buy cigarettes (for they both smoked). Their child was growing up and she also needed things for herself; there were rows and arguments almost every day.

The management at work decided to send him to college for a low voltage jointing course for a month; his wife went home to Germany with their daughter and stayed there for 9 weeks. She did not write to her husband to let him know when she would be coming back to Britain. One day she just phoned him when she was at Victoria Station in London to say he should go to meet them as she had no money to get them to Brighton. William asked her why she did not write to him all the time she was in Germany or inform him that she would be coming back to England but this only caused more arguments. One day a friend who was a Canadian businessman came to visit them and told William he was wasting his time here working for so little money. He advised William to send his wife back to Germany for a short time and to go with him back to Canada. He thought that he would do well there and once he was settled he would send for his wife and daughter. However William refused this offer for he did not want to be separated from his wife and daughter. Although he was having problems and rowing with his wife, he wanted his marriage to work. He continued to work hard and almost all hours to make life comfortable for them. After five years he was asked to go back to college again so he would be able to work on higher voltage. He worked on these for two years and was sent back to college for a management course. After training he became the only man to work on 33,000v at that time.

William and his wife had a neighbour, an old lady called Miss Asals. She liked her own company most of the time and only William could go and speak to her if she wanted something done for her. Miss Asals had no relations in Britain. She was a smart lady but did not like William's wife for she could hear all these rows and she used to see his wife going out and coming back late, sometimes not preparing a meal for the hardworking husband. One day Miss Asals called him to her house and asked him if he would be her executor. He was flattered and agreed. She told him that she was now 70 years old but she would like to live until she was 85 years old. The two carried on being good neighbours to each other but she never talked to his wife.

One day William and his wife had a big row and she left home. Their daughter was now 21 years old, still living at home and training to be a hairdresser, though at that time she wanted to move out to live with her boyfriend. She moved out almost at the same time as her mother. William was a jealous man and it would make him feel sick inside when he used to see his wife flirting. Each time she left home he did not know where she went to, as she had many friends. She did this several times; going away and coming back. He would take her back and for a short time the relationship would be good, but suddenly there would be rows and she would go away again. He was now getting tired of the situation, but he was never a man to cheat on his wife. As long as he was married he would remain true to his marriage vows. What he did not realise was that there was a woman at work who was interested in him. This lady had been transferred from London to work at the Seeboard reception. She started talking to him as he passed through reception and later on they became friends. There was no affair going on between them at the beginning, but Ann knew what she wanted, for left to William it would not have gone further than being friends. Ann was also going through a bad marriage. Her husband was an alcoholic who used to beat her up when he was drunk or wanted money from her for drink. William had never been unfaithful during his married life. When his wife left this time in Easter 1970, Ann invited him to spend the weekend with her at her father's bungalow. William refused to go with her and went home after work to an empty house, as his daughter had left as well as his wife. When he went back to work the next day he said to Ann that he would be pleased to accept the invitation if it was still going. They had two beautiful days together. He had to leave earlier than expected because Ann's friend phoned to tell her that her husband had discharged himself from the hospital where he was drying out. William went back to his house. By now the two were lovers and in love with each other. On the Monday of the following week Ann's husband came to Seeboard as someone had informed him about his wife's affair with William. When he got there he borrowed an intercom and shouted over it saying that a man employed by Seeboard was having an affair with his wife. He wanted the management to hear so that William might be sacked, but he would not go to confront him. Their situation was a difficult one, for they were both still married to their partners, in name only.

William's wife came back; they talked and she wanted to stay with him. She stayed for a few days and at the end of the week when he had gone to work she left taking the whole week's wages. When he came back from work he found his wife gone again, and he went looking for her at her friends' houses. When his wife came home late at night he asked her where she had been; there was a blazing row. Another day he met a friend whom she was supposed to be with and asked her if she and his wife had had a good time. The friend replied she had not seen his wife for a long time, and from that time he was convinced she was seeing other men. Another time she had gone to see his sister, a divorcee with whom she had become firm friends. When William arrived at his sister's house, she came out and told her brother to go away as she would not allow his wife to go back to him; he should go away and not waste their time. He said to his sister that he would never speak to her as long as he lived, and indeed they never communicated with each other for more than thirty years. William blamed himself for introducing his wife to bingo, for from the time she knew how to play she never stopped. She would use all the housekeeping money and it became very difficult to stop her; if he tried to there would be a row. He had taken her there as part of going out for entertainment, for he was not a person to play bingo, and he could not afford to take her out for a meal. They would some times go to a pub for a drink and each time they came home after the pub had closed she would pick a fight. He began to notice that it was an ongoing thing; arguing each time they came home, resulting in sleeping apart. He realised that she was doing it deliberately so that she would not have to share a bed with him.

She left home again, this time taking with her most of their best furniture which they had bought together during their first years of marriage. She then filed for divorce on grounds of mental cruelty. After a few days she came back but would not let him into their bedroom; she would lock the door and he had to sleep in the lounge. William knew that his marriage had ended and although he felt hurt he had no alternative but to accept the situation. He now was waiting for the date to be set for the hearing, and had decided not to contest the divorce. He felt let down in life; he had no one to turn to except at work, where he continued to work even harder. A few weeks went by and one day his wife came back to him, well made-up, as her daughter had done her hair to perfection, and well-dressed, William was quite impressed with her appearance. She sat down and said she had come back for she could not live without him, yet the truth was she had no where to stay. She had exhausted all the friends she had, and William wanted to know why he should take her back and what had changed her mind after she had already filed for a divorce.

A row erupted: he told her that he did not care how smart she looked, he was no longer interested. He had had enough of lies being told to friends and relatives about his cruelty. She stood up and left, and later instructed her lawyers to go ahead with the divorce proceedings. William contacted his lawyers and instructed them that he was not contesting the divorce, and the date was set at the assizes in London. He had to travel all the way to London and when they were called in she was not there. They waited thinking she could have been delayed but after a while they had to adjourn the hearing. William then instructed his lawyers that he would like the next hearing to be held in Brighton for it was expensive for him to travel to London and he was losing money by staying away from work. She did not turn up again at Brighton civil court and on that day William was granted divorce in the absence of his wife. He did not feel any anger against her but hoped that both of them would find happiness in the future. Later he heard that she married someone else.

After a while William went to Ann and informed her that his marriage was over. He asked her if it was not too late could they start again? They both needed each other and their love blossomed, but they did not tell anyone at work that they were in love. They wanted to keep this relationship a secret until they were ready. Ann was still married but to a man who abused her every time they wanted to talk to solve their marriage problems. One evening he beat her up and after that he just went and flopped on the sofa and within a short time he was snoring away deep in sleep. Ann had locked herself in the bedroom with her dog which was very protective of its mistress, then phoned William to tell him about the beating, and that she was scared that if her husband woke up he might start beating her again. She asked him to go there and help her to move to her friend's. When William arrived she climbed out through the window with two bags containing her few belongings and went to stay with her friend and William went back to his home. When Ann's husband woke up early in the morning he tried to open the bedroom door but it was locked. When he went outside he saw that the window was open and there was no one inside.

One day William took Ann to show her where he lived. They stopped outside and Ann said she would love to live in a house rather than a bungalow. He replied that if ever the house went on sale he would buy it, for as a sitting tenant he had the first refusal. One day he asked Ann to come and live with him, as he was now divorced, and so they started living together. On the first day she moved in she sat down and cried about the home she had left and how lucky she was to have met a man who appreciated her as a woman.

At that time the owner of the house was an old lady who was in hospital. When she died her friends and relations came to the house and took away most of her personal effects. William was waiting patiently to hear what was going to be done about the house, and it was not long before it was put on sale. The house was in the best area of Hove and most people who lived there were thought to be comfortably off. One day Ann received a letter from a relation informing her that her father was seriously ill with emphysema and shingles. William took her to see him and to take him to the doctor, and the doctor decided to get him into hospital. After two days he died. After the funeral their father's bungalow was put up for sale and the two daughters shared the proceeds, each daughter getting £6,000. William after some time phoned the solicitor who was dealing with the sale of his house to say that he wanted to buy it. The solicitor told him that he would be sending a property agent to discuss the sale with him as a sitting tenant. When the agent came he asked what price William was prepared to pay which would be reasonable to both parties. He offered £7,000 but both agreed on £8,250. He accepted the offer and the solicitor arranged the mortgage for him. When Ann received the money from the sale of her father's bungalow she gave William £4,000 to pay towards their house leaving them with £4,250 to pay.

Ann later started divorce proceedings against her husband. He refused to give her a divorce although he knew that his wife was now living with another man. He was now sitting in their bungalow drinking away his life and all the money she had left. Her solicitor advised her to fight for the bungalow, but she refused as she thought he would suffer if he had nowhere to live. One day her husband suddenly agreed to go to court for the hearing and Ann's solicitor advised him to go through with the divorce, he agreed.

William and Ann continued to live together without marriage. William wanted to be sure that she loved him as much as he loved her, and did not want to rush. At the moment they were very happy with each other, and he thought a piece of paper would not change anything; they were living as husband and wife. A year later Ann in a way proposed, as she said to him that she would very much like to be married to him. He was very pleased to hear this and they went out to celebrate their engagement. Later they started to think of getting married at the registry office. They had to have witnesses so Ann asked a friend whom she had confided in about their relationship and William asked Miss Asals their neighbour who was very pleased that William had found a lovely lady at last. So they were married with their two witnesses but they still wanted no one at work to know that they were married, and William never told his daughter about his marriage. One day they attended a funeral of a colleague at work and as they arrived at the funeral together a lot of people looked at them accusingly as if they were having an affair. Still they kept it quiet for another year, but obviously all secrets do come out. When the manager found out he was not amused and demanded to know why he was not told of this marriage. He met William later and congratulated him, and gave him £2 for a bottle of wine. The money was not from his pocket but from the office petty cash which was kept for emergencies. William thanked him but in his heart he was amused by it all. Now everyone at work knew that they were a couple and had been married for a year, the situation was more relaxed and there was no more whispering in the office that they were living in sin. William continued to help out their neighbour with little jobs that needed doing, and she trusted only him to go into her house and speak to her. Ann would also speak to her if they saw each other outside for she liked Ann, but she was a lady of very few words.

Ann wanted to stop working because she had started to feel unwell. They discussed it, but William was worried that if she stopped working they would have a difficult time paying their mortgage on one person's wages. He begged her to work for a while longer. After a few weeks a friend at work spoke to William about his wife and said that she was not well. So he said to his wife that she should stop working if she was not well and Ann left work and became a fulltime housewife. Later on he enjoyed coming home and finding his wife waiting for him after a long day. Now that Ann was at home she had time to talk more with their neighbour Miss Asals. They would go out, but not every day; they would attend company clubs and sometimes invite their friends to their home. William and Ann were a very happy couple. They had both come from unhappy marriages and were enjoying each other's company and a wonderful marriage which they had each thought was never going to happen to them. William's hobby was gardening and Ann enjoyed cooking. They both agreed that they would not have children as he was in his late forties and she was only six years younger and not in good health. They decided that he should have a vasectomy; that way they would be sure she would not become pregnant.

William and Ann always used to go to Wales for their holidays. They had a dog which they never wanted to leave in kennels, as he was never happy to be left behind even for a short time. He was a joy to them. Ann was not well but she was not a person to complain about her pain and fears. One year when they were in Wales she became so unwell that they had to return home. She had not been able to open her bowels for two weeks and immediately they got home she went to see her doctor and was soon sent to the hospital for investigations. At the hospital they waited ten hours to be attended to by a doctor, and when later Ann was examined she was prepared for surgery as an emergency case. She stayed in hospital for a few days and after her discharge she was well and began to enjoy life again. For two years she had no illness, but one day she was rushed to the hospital with the same complaint and another operation was performed. After that she became well again and they went for another holiday in Wales. After a few days in Wales having a wonderful time and happy that Ann was feeling better recuperating from the surgery, William received a telephone message that his father had died. Ann asked if he wanted to go to the funeral, for she was prepared to go, but knowing that she could not bear another long drive back home for she was still feeling weak, he decided to stay until the end of their holiday. She felt very sad about this for she blamed herself that her husband could not attend his father's funeral. He was still bitter towards his father whom he had not seen for a long time after their disagreements, so he left the funeral arrangements to his stepmother.

After their holiday Ann appeared to be doing well for a time. Miss Asals spoke to William over their adjoining hedge after he had been back a few days and told him that she was not feeling well. He insisted that she should go and see her doctor, and offered to call a doctor for her, but she declined. She said she did not want to see a doctor as she was not all that ill and going to get better, but she promised that if she did not feel better in a few days she would call a doctor. Life went on smoothly for a few years as Ann was feeling well and Miss Asals was not complaining of any pain; but one day Miss Asals told William that she was not feeling well again and that she wanted to see a doctor. He immediately phoned for him and she was taken to the hospital. William was the only person to visit her as she had no family except a brother who emigrated to America as a young man. She was later discharged from the hospital and seemed to be doing well.

After a few weeks Ann woke William up and said to him he must go and check on Miss Asals as she had a funny feeling that all was not well next door. He had her spare key so he could go in to check on things if she was not there. Ann followed him into the house and found her on the floor with her head a foot away from the fire. They sat her up and called her doctor who came and examined her and said there was nothing wrong with her. After her fall a week went by and she became unwell again and was rushed to the hospital. She was given a private room and she liked that, for she was a very private person. They would visit her every day and her eyes would light up when she saw them. She was like a little girl happy to see her parents. One day when they visited her they found that she was not in bed. They were frantic for they thought she had died, but a nurse told them that she had been transferred to a specialist hospital for chest problems. They went to visit her there; she looked ill and her condition had deteriorated. After a few days she became unconscious. They continued to go and see her every day, but one day William received a telephone call when he was at work from the hospital to say that Miss Asals had died. Because she had named him as her executor they wanted to know about the funeral arrangements. He went to the hospital but they refused to let him see the body. He then went home for he needed to go into her house to look through her papers. When they went into her house and started to look through her papers they felt as if they were intruding into her affairs. They found out that she was a very methodical person, everything was neat and well-organised. They found the solicitor's name and address and when they went through the pile of documents they found a copy of her will.

Ann started to read the will only to find that she had left everything she possessed to William (I leave everything to my dear friend; two houses, one in London and the one in Brighton next door to him). They were both shocked and happy at the same time. They just sat down for they could not take it in. They went through the drawers for they still thought there could be another will leaving her property to her brother, but there was no other will, and they found four hundred pounds in the drawer. William soon after that phoned her brother in America and informed him of his sister's death. He thanked him for letting him know and said he would be sending twenty pounds to buy flowers for the funeral. He told William that he was 85 years old now and would not be travelling to Britain for the funeral. A few days after the funeral William took the will to Miss Asals' solicitor. Although it had been witnessed by two people, because she had not signed on the dotted line but in a different place, the solicitor told him that the will was invalid. William and Ann were disappointed but took comfort from the thought that they had not lost anything which belonged to them, only something they never had. They stood up and thanked the solicitor for his time and were just about to go when he asked them to sit down while he talked to his senior partner about the signature. He came back to tell them that it was valid after all.

William never liked London, so the first thing he did was to sell the house he had inherited in London for thirty thousand pounds. Then he and Ann started to renovate the house next door into a holiday apartment upstairs and downstairs into a garage for their car. They were now property owners and had a comfortable life, still going for their holidays to North Wales.

After two years Ann went into hospital with the same abdominal complaint as before. She was operated on and had to have an ileostomy. After that life went on as usual without problems, until one day she started to show a slight vaginal bleed. She went to her doctor and was sent to hospital for tests. It was found that she had a malignant tumour. She was operated on on Good Friday, but returning to the ward started bleeding so profusely that they could not stop it and had to be taken back to theatre on Easter Sunday. She stayed in hospital for four weeks and was discharged with a permanent colostomy. Unfortunately they had been unable to remove all of the tumour as it was deep-seated, but they would wait till she was strong enough to stand another operation. Although William was not happy about this there was nothing he could do but to wait as advised. At home he had to learn to cope with changing a colostomy bag, for Ann was very weak.The medical team had not offered him counselling, or shown him how to change the bag. It was a very traumatic situation for both him and Ann, but he learnt quickly and became quite good at it. After some time and with good nursing care from her husband she got a little better, until one day she told him that she wanted to enjoy her life with him for she did not want to die yet. Then after two years she told William she was not feeling well and he said to her, oh no not again. He called his dog and went for a long walk in the hills, thinking to himself how unfair life was. When he came back he took her in his arms; nothing was said in words but he was thinking he should not have said, oh no not again. He did not mean to say why was she doing that again what he meant was, oh no it was not happening to us again when we thought everything was fine. But Ann had phoned her friend when he was out and told her that he was very upset, and that she thought this time it had really got to him. At work William had been asked to retire; he was now fifty-eight years old, but he refused for he thought he was still young and enjoyed his work. The management agreed that he should stay on, but after some time they asked him again to retire on more money and a good pension. As Ann was ill again he thought it would be a good idea to be with her at home. He could do his garden as well as looking after his wife, so he agreed on the condition that if his wife died he would not be retired.

William then retired, and he and Ann again had a good time together, without him having to go to work, and he came to realise that he was enjoying his free time. Ann went into hospital for tests and was told she had no cancer, or at any rate they could find none. They celebrated by booking holidays abroad to Turkey, Madeira and Corfu, and for three years they had a wonderful life together. When they were on one of their holidays abroad, Ann complained of abdominal pain and diarrhoea. They ran out of colostomy bags to Ann's great embarrassment but luckily they were staying in a holiday apartment and were alone. William helped her to clean up the mess. When they came home she went into hospital but was discharged the next day for the problem had cleared up. She was a strong person who never complained or wished to worry her husband. The following month however, she admitted that she had pain and seeing that she was not looking well William called the doctor who in turn called immediately for an ambulance. Ann was put on intravenous fluids with a tube down her throat for aspiration as she could not hold any food down. In the meantime she was waiting for the result of tests to ascertain the cause of her vomiting. William had a talk with one of the surgeons on the team investigating her problem, who said he would have to operate; for it could be cancer. After the operation they were told that there was no cancer, the tubes were removed and she felt better. After three or four days, she felt dazed and confused and completely lost her memory for three days. On the tenth day after the operation she could not walk properly, blood was taken for more tests and it was found that she was severely anaemic. She was becoming more ill by the day. Blood transfusion was commenced and after two days William was told she could go home. He was not happy about taking her home when she was so ill, so he went to talk to the doctor and told him that Ann was not well enough to be discharged, for by now she was not aware of what day or time it was, but the doctor said she would settle when she got home. She stayed in the hospital that night, but when William went home he got a call from the hospital saying that she was very ill and he should go back. On arrival he was told that she had a blood clot in her lung and was now on oxygen; more tests were done, and he was told that the medical team had decided that there was nothing more they could do for his wife. Two days later she was still on oxygen, but the doctor emphasised that she was looking much better and was fit enough to go home in two days. William did not think so, for she looked very ill. After two days she was discharged and sent home by ambulance. At home she looked really ill and there was nothing he could do about it but to try and make his wife as comfortable as he could.

He was devastated and kept asking himself why they had done this to her. Was it because they knew she was dying, and if so why did they not tell him, rather than keeping him hoping that she would be all right? A district nurse came to see Ann and found her very ill indeed. She contacted the general practitioner who decided to send her back to hospital. On admission this time they did a scan. The results were that she had cancer of the colon which had metastasised; that is, the cancer had spread all over her body. She was beyond treatment. So much time had been wasted by not finding out earlier what was wrong. The doctor whom William had spoken to before said that he had thought that she had cancer. William asked why he had not told him earlier – why did he let him keep on hoping for the best when he thought all the time that she had cancer? The surgeon had no answer to that. Ann stayed in the hospital for about two weeks; she had now had a stroke and was paralysed on one side. She was being given medication to lessen the swelling in her brain and lungs. She was then discharged on that medication, but William was still fighting for his wife's life. He went to another surgeon and begged him to operate on his wife to remove the tumour, and offered to pay – money was no problem to him if it meant that the tumour would be removed and she would be all right again. This surgeon's secretary informed William privately that he should not waste his money, for he would not be doing anything different from the NHS doctors. William must just make his wife comfortable and spend as much time as he could with her, love and make her as happy as he could. He went away and asked himself, was this the National Health Service which people have to depend on? For a person to go through all that pain and suffering before anything could be done was very bad.

William now looked after Ann at home, with visits from health visitors. He was very protective of his wife and would not let anyone touch her. He had put a bed in the lounge downstairs, as she was now unable to climb the stairs, and would sit with her until she went to sleep. In the morning he would get up wash her, change the colostomy bag and empty the urine bag. After that he would cook and feed her then make her comfortable before he had his breakfast. A friend offered to cook small meals for them, for sometimes he would not be able to cook as well as cleaning the house. Ann was now on a diamorphine syringe driver pump to reduce pain. At times he would take his wife for a drive just to get her out for some fresh air, but she would tire very easily and lose interest. During her last days she did not want anyone coming to visit them. She wanted her husband to herself, and would be unhappy if her friends came and he talked to them. At times he was beside himself as he was almost cut off from the outside world. He had no relation or friend to talk to, not only about his problems but just about everyday life. He never became cross with her, even though he was becoming a very lonely man. His daughter had stopped talking to her father, for she had not liked the woman he had married and Ann had not liked her. One day during Ann's last days he went to let his daughter know that his wife was very ill and that she could die at any time; he was seeking support and sympathy.

On the 27th October 1993 William woke up as usual, washed, fed and made Ann comfortable. Then he sat with his arms around her, and as he sat with his wife he heard a small sigh, and knew that his beloved had died. Later, when it sank in that she really had died and he was now alone, he thought there was nothing to live for and sometimes contemplated going to throw himself off Beachy Head. Friends told him that that was a cowardly way of getting out of one's problems and that time is a great healer. He would not forget the times they had together.